POEMS OF
ANDRÉ BRETON

A BILINGUAL ANTHOLOGY

translated & edited by

JEAN-PIERRE CAUVIN
MARY ANN CAWS

BLACK
WIDOW
PRESS

BOSTON, MASS.

Poems of André Breton
A Bilingual Anthology

Black Widow Press edition, second printing, March 2014

Joseph S. Phillips and Susan J. Wood, Ph.D., Publishers

ISBN-13: 978-0-9768449-2-1
ISBN-10: 0-9768449-2-3

Library of Congress Cataloging-in-Publication Data

Breton, André, 1896–1966.
    [Poems. English & French. Selections]
    Poems of André Breton : a bilingual anthology / translated & edited by Jean-Pierre Cauvin, Mary Ann Caws.— 1st ed.
    p. cm.
    Includes bibliographical references.
    ISBN-13: 978-0-9768449-2-1 (alk. paper)
    1. Breton, André, 1896-1966—Translations into English. I. Cauvin, Jean Pierre. II. Caws, Mary Ann. III. Title.

PQ2603.R35A23 2006
841'.914—dc22

2006002729

Printed in the United States

10   9   8   7   6   5   4   3   2

POEMS
of André Breton

Contents

Preface: In the Surrealist Light: André Breton, *Mary Ann Caws* 1

Introduction: The Poethics of André Breton, *Jean-Pierre Cauvin* 11

FROM *MONT DE PIÉTÉ* (1919)

Age [Age] 38–39

Pour Lafcadio [For Lafcadio] 40–41

Monsieur V [Monsieur V] 42–43

Une Maison peu solide [An Unsteady House] 44–45

Le Corset Mystère [The Mystery Corset] 46–47

FROM *CLAIR DE TERRE* (1923)

Amour parcheminé [Love in Parchment] 50–51

Cartes sur les dunes [Cards on the Dunes] 52–53

« C'est aussi le bagne ... » ["It too is the penitentiary..."] 54–55

Rendez-vous [Rendez-vous] 56–57

Privé [Private] 58–59

Le Buvard de cendre [Cinder Blotter] 60–61

Tout paradis n'est pas perdu [No Paradise is Lost] 62–63

Silhouette de paille [Straw Silhouette] 64–65

Mille et mille fois [A Thousand Times and More] 66–69

Ligne brisée [Broken Line] 70–73

Tournesol [Sunflower] 74–75

FROM *POISSON SOLUBLE* (1924)

« Moins de temps ... » ["Less time..."] 78–79

« Sale nuit, nuit de fleurs ... » ["Night of filth, night of flowers..."] 80–81

« On s'est avisé ... » ["One day someone..."] 82–85

« Il y avait ... » ["There was once..."] 86–87

L'UNION LIBRE (1931)

L'Union libre [Free Union] 90–93

FROM *LE REVOLVER À CHEVEUX BLANCS* (1932)

Non-lieu [No Grounds]   96–97

Le Verbe être [The Verb To Be]   98–99

La Forêt dans la hache [The Forest in the Axe]   100–101

Toutes les écolières ensemble
[All the Schoolgirls Together]   102–103

Nœud des miroirs [Knot of Mirrors]   104–107

Facteur Cheval [Postman Cheval]   108–111

Rideau rideau [Curtain Curtain]   112–115

Le Sphinx vertébral [The Vertebral Sphinx]   116–119

Vigilance [Vigilance]   120–121

Sans connaissance [Unconscious]   122–127

Une Branche d'ortie entre par la fenêtre [A Stalk of
Nettle Enters through the Window]   128–129

Le Grand Secours meurtrier [Deadly Rescue]   130–131

FROM *L'AIR DE L'EAU* (1934)

« Monde dans un baiser » ["World in a kiss"]   134–135

« Je rêve je te vois ... » ["Dreaming I see you..."]   136–137

« Le Marquis de Sade a regagné l'intérieur ... » ["The
Marquis de Sade has gone back inside..."]   138–139

Au beau demi-jour [In the lovely twilight]   140–143

« Yeux zinzolins ... " ["Zinnia-red eyes..."]   144–145

« Il allait être cinq heures du matin »
["It was about to be five in the morning"]   146–147

« Ils vont tes membres ... » ["Your limbs go
unfolding..."]   148–149

« A ta place ... » ["If I were you..."]   150–151

« Toujours pour la première fois » ["Always for the
first time"]   152–155

On me dit [They tell me]   156–157

FROM *1935–1940* (in *Poèmes*, 1948)

Monde [World]   160–161

Le Puits enchanté [The Enchanted Well]   162–167

Cours-les toutes [Run-them-all]   168–173

Quels apprêts [What Frills]   174–177

FATA MORGANA (1940)
    Fata Morgana [Fata Morgana]   180–203

FROM 1940–1943 (in Poèmes, 1948)
    Frôleuse [Flirt]   206–209
    Passage à niveau [Grade Crossing]   210–211
    Premiers transparents [Transparent Firsts]   212–213
    Plus que suspect [More than Suspect]   214–215
    Intérieur [Interior]   216–217
    Guerre [War]   218–221

FROM LES ÉTATS GÉNÉRAUX (1948)
    « Dis ce qui est dessous ... »
    ["Say what is underneath..."]   224–227

FROM DES ÉPINGLES TREMBLANTES (1948)
    La Lanterne sourde [The Dark Lantern]   230–231

FROM XÉNOPHILES (1948)
    « La nuit en Haïti ... » ["In Haiti at night..."]   234–235
    Korwar [Korwar]   236–237
    Uli [Uli]   238–239
    Dukduk [Dukduk]   240–241
    Tiki [Tiki]   242–243
    Rano Raraku [Rano Raraku]   244–245

FROM OUBLIÉS (1948)
    Ecoute au coquillage [Seashell Sail]   248–249
    Sur la route de San Romano [On the Road to
       San Romano]   250–253

FROM CONSTELLATIONS (1959)
    Personnages dans la nuit guidés par les traces
       phosphorescentes des escargots [Persons in the
       Night Guided by Phosphorescent Snail Tracks]   256–257
    Femmes sur la plage [Women on the Beach]   258–259

*Femme à la blonde aisselle coiffant sa chevelure
à la lueur des étoiles* [Woman with Blond
Underarm Combing Her Hair in the Starlight]   260–261

L'Etoile matinale [Morning Star]   262–263

Personnage blessé [Injured Person]   264–265

Le Chant du rossignol à minuit et la pluie matinale
[The Song of the Nightingale at Midnight and
the Morning Rain]   266–267

Le Réveil au petit jour [The Awakening at Daybreak]   268–269

*Femmes au bord d'un lac à la surface irisée par le
passage d'un cygne* [Women by the Shore of a
Lake Made Iridescent by a Passing Swan]   270–271

*Le Bel Oiseau déchiffrant l'inconnu au couple
d'amoureux* [The Lovely Bird Deciphering
the Unknown for a Pair of Lovers]   272–273

FROM *LE LA* (1961)
«*La 'dictée de la pensée'* ... » ["The experience
(active-passive) of listening..."]   276–277

Notes   279

Notes on the Poems   282
The Life and Works of André Breton   296

Selected Bibliography   301

Key to Translators
(JPC)—Jean Pierre Cauvin
(MAC)—Mary Ann Caws
(MAC/PT)—Mary Ann Caws & Patricia Terry
no designation—Jean Pierre Cauvin & Mary Ann Caws jointly

Photomatons of André Breton taken in 1925. Reproduced courtesy of Humanities Research Center, The University of Texas at Austin.

PREFACE

In the Surrealist Light:
André Breton

Mary Ann Caws

ndré Breton was the greatest surrealist of them all; even if his poems had no intrinsic "literary" value in themselves, they would be the valued witnesses to an epoch, a movement, an attitude. But the present selections are not intended to be inscribed in a single school or perceived from a single optic; their complex interrelations with other texts and with the visual universe, passionately arrived at, circumvent any isolating tactic.

The translations of these poems themselves have a double goal, both accuracy within the composition and the attempt to keep the atmosphere of the original. That atmosphere is not itself always "poetic," if that term is taken to mean lyric, self-reflective, self-contained, or appealing: these poems are often and deliberately uneven, ungraceful, obscure. They can be luminous without being intelligible, magnetizing while not attractive in the ordinary sense. We have tried to choose the most illuminating poems as well as the most representative ones, from different periods and different styles, offering various perspectives corresponding to the multiple approaches Breton, and surrealism, took over the years.

As some indication of the complexity of Breton's universe, we might briefly consider the echoes and the postures and mirrorings, the costumes, the role-playing and the play of images. One of the more revealing titles is the early *Mont de Piété* [Pawnshop], for these texts are indeed often composed of borrowings and resettings, as heteroclite objects make a brilliant bric-a-brac. Surrealism trades this for that, making of the exchange itself a work of art. In the early poems, these objects, for example *The Mystery Corset*, take precedence over what we might think of as the "human" as well as the formal aspects of the text, whereas later, their profusion is subdued, for greater emotional and poetic effect. As for the anecdotal interest, and other references to the exterior, we give in the notes only the most essential clarifications, believing in the self-contained, and frequently self-referring, quality of the text. Not that our attitude is "neutral" or objective: the intensity of surrealism demands a like response, passionate in kind.

Just as the title *Mont de piété* indicates the juxtapositions and convergences of objects, those of sight and those of desire, Breton's titles often indicate not only his states of mind but the basic tenets of surrealism itself: such expressions as *L'Air de l'eau* [Airwater] and *Clair de terre* [Earthlight] suggest in their composite formation the surrealist hope placed in the juxtaposition of two elements, of two states or two things, eventually and eternally crossing over one into the other, as *clair de lune* [moonlight] crosses light with night, the luminous with the obscure. Here the surrealist takes the initial set phrase or the accepted cliché, *clair de lune,* and reconditions it. We might examine, in the light of this technique, a highly significant expression, paradoxical to the extreme, from one of Breton's poems, *Toujours pour la première fois,* "always for the first time." It is, I think, this "first time" that gives exceptional value to the convergence, seen rapidly and rapidly transcribed. The paradox enhances the intensity of the psychological and poetic effect: surrealism is meant to be, and is, *striking.* Pierre Reverdy's notion of the image giving off its fullest light when it is the product of two elements clashing, as they are taken from distant fields and juxtaposed, finds its fullest realization in Breton, who acknowledges Reverdy as the source of this notion so important in surrealist thought.[1] The spark struck by the meeting of opposites clarifies by its brilliance the dullest of everyday perceptions, infusing it with the light of the marvelous. The perception precedes the remaking of the world, but the latter is indeed—for the surrealists—remade as it is reseen. Following the same train of thought, we might consider that the retranslation of a poem is the recreation of it: Breton would not have disagreed.

As language is to remake the universe, the power of speech deter-mines both existing and knowing: "Thought is made in the mouth," said Tristan Tzara,[2] and Breton goes a step further. "Man is soluble in his thought"[3]: thus the image of a dissolving fish, undone and created by its own element. *Poisson soluble.* And so the titles continue to indicate the mental attitude on which the texts are predicated: *Le Revolver à cheveux blancs* [The White-Haired Revolver] exemplifies the clash of contraries, for the white smoke coming forth makes a powerful visual reminder of an elderly man and, in conjunction with the fire potential in the weapon, typifies the clash between age and youth's fiery temper: both meanings are implicit, held in tension within the title, just as the best surrealist writing holds in tension its ambivalences, consciously and vigorously. That so many of the word plays of surrealist poetry have to be differently captured in translation is not to be grieved over, for the very shifts and switches enable the fresh reading which should keep the poetry alive, exactly as it does not serve the cause of prosaic consistency.

Surrealist poetry never serves: this is another matter of conscience. The poem from *Le Revolver à cheveux blancs* called "Non-lieu" [No Grounds], for instance, insists upon the concept of freedom as unusable except in its own limits:

Jamais la liberté que pour la liberté

[Never freedom except for freedom]

The texts of the movement, untamed in their own motion, development, and space, are to be given free rein, but nothing can be expected or predicted of them. This poetry at its summit is likely to celebrate, as Breton does, not a smooth domesticated tissue of images in a neat system and an untroubled text, but a barbaric flame, racing the length of a text as of a life, until the final extraordinary convergence of one element with its opposite, a convergence toward which the reading projects all its haste and passion, its optimistic meeting and active joining:

Flamme d'eau guide-moi jusqu'à la mer de feu[4]

[Flame of water guide me to the sea of fire]

Such convergence provides for the elements the same kind of "free union" that Breton claims for the ideal love of man and woman in *L'Amour fou* [Mad Love], the overwhelming because irrational emotion of the marvelous encounter to which many of his works are dedicated. The contraries flower in their meeting, and spread out from the individual toward the cosmic, in a totalizing figure, set under the sign of a final liquid image:

Tout le pommier en fleur de la mer[5]

[The whole flowering apple tree of the sea]

The framing of Breton's poetry is as powerful as the imagery itself, both the initiation into and the exit out of the text exhibiting visible signals. For example, the two exemplary convergences quoted above are realized in the concluding lines of the poems from which they are quoted: many of Breton's major poems are meliorative in sense, opening out from the initial line, often announcing some stage or poem set befitting the marvelous of "everyday life," in a crescendo building toward the final perception of a universe remarkably changed for the better, for the more hopeful and for the greater, to which one culminating final image of passionate encounter often bears witness, in an expansion and explosion of a single line.

Now no one would claim that all the texts of surrealism are hopeful ones; of the particularities of that movement, or as I prefer to think of it, of that attitude, one of the most essential is its double nature, clearly expressed in its poetics, and in the many proliferating images of a positive duplicity, such as all those we might term « l'envers et l'endroit »: the right and the wrong side, the upper and the under weave, transposed into images of a door swinging in or out, a dream encountered in daylight or light within the dark of a dream, the rise and falling of the poetic path, in all the revelation of language opening upon the world. Surrealist lyricism—and here it is well to remember that one of Breton's definitions of surrealism is that of a *lyric comportment*—is frequently found in just the deliberately surprising dichotomy of bright and dark, high and low, as was Dada lyricism before.[6] To take a text as an instance, « Le Verbe être » [The Verb To Be], a prose poem from *Le Revolver à cheveux blancs,* presents a vision of despair and exaltation within one long paragraph of celebration. It is composed of deformed clichés *(la mer à boire,* "the sea to drink," turned into the rhyming expression *un verre à boire,* "a drinking glass," thus recalling the former expression which it reduces to the size of one small glass from which to drink both being and the world), those deformations then reformed into poetry. All the humor of repetition and mockery and even the central theme of despair and the pictures it entails, one after the other, help to form a dense, complex, and powerful text in which the most heterogeneous images are valorized in themselves and given equal weight and an equally ambivalent interpretation: thus the table cleared by the seaside conveys both the tragic and necessary removal or sweeping away of the past and the optimistic openness to the future of, literally, a *tabula rasa.* The final ambiguity, resuming the whole by a quantity, unspecified, of "days fewer which will again make up my life," brings us out on the side of the living, as the fewer accumulate somehow into the greater, the more into the less. The reversal of ordinary expectations contributes to the emotional charge of the poem, building up exactly as it seems to diminish.

The interchange of elements, always essential in surrealism, finds its fullest discussion, political, psychological, and personal, in the volume *Les Vases communicants* [Communicating Vessels], at the conclusion of which a formerly private and magical muse shakes out her hair in the brightest of daylights, as secrecy and sharing, intimacy and exposure, dark and clarity merge. The universe of surrealism is adapted to this orientation: by the burning end of the poem "Vigilance" (in *Le Revolver à cheveux blancs*), like a watch kept faithfully over the whole of life for the benefit of boundless freedom, the narrator, confronted with his own exposed and sleeping body laid out, commits a violent act upon his own being, a total consumption of the human:

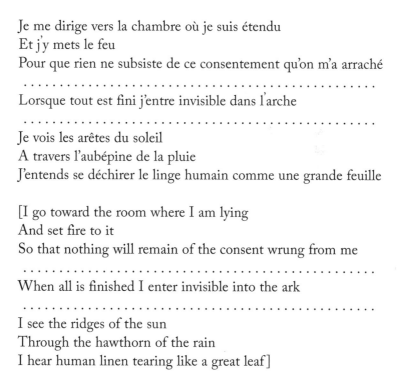

Je me dirige vers la chambre où je suis étendu
Et j'y mets le feu
Pour que rien ne subsiste de ce consentement qu'on m'a arraché
. . . .
Lorsque tout est fini j'entre invisible dans l'arche
. . . .
Je vois les arêtes du soleil
A travers l'aubépine de la pluie
J'entends se déchirer le linge humain comme une grande feuille

[I go toward the room where I am lying
And set fire to it
So that nothing will remain of the consent wrung from me
. . . .
When all is finished I enter invisible into the ark
. . . .
I see the ridges of the sun
Through the hawthorn of the rain
I hear human linen tearing like a great leaf]

Here the final convergence of the marvelous is attained, within the grasp of the poet who has found the center, summing it up for us all, in the thread of one single line:

Je ne touche plus que le cœur des choses je tiens le fil

[I touch nothing but the heart of things I hold the thread]

No more than this line is needed, for it forms at once the initial impulse and the central link of the whole fabric of encounter, never smooth, always to be challenged and rewoven.

At this point elements can mingle as in *L'Air de l'eau,* a collection in which Breton's surrealist vision reaches an emotional peak. Images are no longer simply convergent, horizontally and vertically: they are rather multiplied and superimposed one upon the other:

Je rêve je te vois superposée indéfiniment à toi-même

[I dream I see your image indefinitely imposed upon itself]

Geographical limits transgressed, together with the mindless separations of age: child/woman, and category: human/mermaid or goddess, single/multiple, and even French/Italian mark the mythological world, no less real for its references which extend beyond the particular to the shared:

Tu es assise sur le haut tabouret de corail
Devant ton miroir[7] toujours à son premier quartier
Deux doigts sur l'aile d'eau du peigne
Et en même temps
Tu reviens de voyage tu t'attardes la dernière dans la grotte.[8]
. . . .
Tu es étendue sur le lit tu t'éveilles ou tu t'endors
Tu t'éveilles où tu t'es endormie ou ailleurs
. . . .
Et la même
Enfant
. . . .
Ma fontaine vivante de Sivas

[You are seated on the high coral stool
Before your mirror still in its first quarter
Two fingers on the water wing of the comb

And at the same time
You return from your travels you are the last to linger in the
  grotto

· ·

You are lying on the bed you awaken or you fall asleep
You awaken where you fell asleep or elsewhere

· ·

And the same
Child

· ·

My living fountain of Shiva]

Now the celebration of what surrealism calls "the sublime point" is always joined to preceding acts of homage and is yet always new, constant whatever the changing exterior reference, from *L'Amour fou* as the poetic treatise on inspired and irrational love, to *Arcane 17*, tinged with mysticism, from the child-woman "singing always in the imagination of man"[9] like Melusina, fairy and mortal, Morgan Le Fay or Breton's *Fata Morgana*, and from alchemical sister to mistress and muse. The figures merge, in our repeated readings which would choose at their and our best, to include all possible interpretations and ambivalences. Surrealism is the art of the possible.

Surrealism, finally, merges the contraries, confronts the ordinary with the arcane, the systematic with the thrown-together, like the initially raw and diverse material of our various lives, from which poetry is to be made. Fortunately, in that poetry, as in those lives, a great deal will always remain unexplained and uncaught:

On ne saurait décrire en art
L'engin à prendre le renard bleu[10]

[In art one can hardly describe
The device for catching the blue fox]

INTRODUCTION
The Poethics of André Breton

Jean-Pierre Cauvin

Après vous, mon beau langage.
[After you, my lovely language.]

—Breton, « Introduction au Discours
sur le peu de réalité »

Any attempt at defining the poetry of André Breton must begin with mention of a notion for which there unfortunately exists no corresponding term in English, and that is the notion of *dépaysement:* the sense of being out of one's element, of being disoriented in the presence of the uncanny, or disconcerted by the unfamiliarity of a situation experienced for the first time. Without *dépaysement,* there is no *merveilleux,* no encounter with the marvelous, the objective of all surrealist activity. Both terms imply a subversion of accepted norms and values, a reevaluation of reality— at least of reality as defined in Western culture. At its inception and in all its later phases, surrealism aims at revolutionizing our experience of words and of things by stripping them of their conventionality, their banality, and their utilitarian purpose, the better to foster the emergence of the unknown and the unexpected that lie dormant within their everyday appearance. For the surrealists in general and Breton in particular, it is the privilege, indeed the mission, of poetry to liberate the immense potential of the human psyche by repudiating the forces of reason and routine which hold it in check. Poetry is not art, but life itself, life as a constant adventure shepherded by chance, love, and liberty. Life is poetry in practice, the pursuit of adventure « dans le langage, dans la rue, ou dans le rêve »[1] [in language, in the street, or in dreams]. Poetry entails a radical transformation of the self and of society. All human concerns fall within its purview: psychological, ethical, and material. Like the alchemical quest, poetry seeks to transmute into the gold of a better life all the elements of mind and matter. The sensuous and intellectual desiderata of traditional poetry—euphony, lyricism, verbal virtuosity, elegance of discourse, taste—and the formal or structural devices it prescribes are, for Breton, the trappings of an outworn literature designed to charm, to reassure, and to please. His disdain for composition, rhyme, and rhythm is matched by his rejection of the poetics of transcendence so prevalent in nineteenth-century literature. In this regard, Breton's loyalties lie with Rimbaud and Lautréamont (Isidore Ducasse), two revolutionaries whose present-day importance can in no small measure be attributed to his lifelong advocacy of their works. Breton's own poetry thus constitutes an anti-poetics, all the more because it unfailingly disregards formal concerns: « La poésie? elle n'est pas où on la croit. Elle existe en dehors des mots, du style, etc. »² ["Poetry? It isn't where you think. It exists outside of words, of style, etc."] The subversion of poetic form is of course a consequence of Breton's war on reason. Because its function is to police and to censor, to reduce and to exclude, reason's participation in the poetic act is negative. By superimposing form and convention upon the spontaneous and the inchoate, reason conceals. The role of poetry, on the other hand, is to reveal. Poetry is nothing less than the antithesis of repressive reason and the translation of desire (the energizing principle of the unconscious and a key word in the Bretonian lexicon). The surrealist poetic act is not a function of poetics, but of what I shall call *poethics:* it bespeaks a way of life. Inasmuch as art implies premeditation, the notion of literature as art no longer obtains. The overriding objective of surrealist activity is precisely to eliminate any interference by the mind's rational, conscious processes in order to eavesdrop on the unrehearsed murmur of the unconscious. Like Baudelaire before him, Breton believed that the most precious endowment of the human mind is the imagination. The play of involuntary images constituting the language of the unconscious is the most genuine manifestation of the vital forces within us—forces whose inherent logic cannot be equated with that of our conscious intellect. By tapping the wellsprings of the imagination, we can achieve a deeper knowledge—knowledge of the surreal, synonymous with the marvelous. Clearly, the least-expected images are the most "marvelous," as unconditioned spontaneity alone confers significance upon them:

> Pour moi, [l'image] la plus forte est celle qui présente le degré d'arbitraire le plus élevé . . . ; celle qu'on met le plus longtemps à traduire en langage pratique, soit qu'elle recèle une dose énorme de contradiction apparente, soit que l'un de ses termes en soit curieusement dérobé, soit que s'annonçant sensationnelle, elle ait l'air de se dénouer faiblement . . . , soit qu'elle tire d'elle-même une justification *formelle* dérisoire, soit qu'elle soit d'ordre hallucinatoire, soit qu'elle prête très naturellement à l'abstrait, le masque du concret, ou inversement, soit qu'elle implique la négation de quelque propriété physique élémentaire, soit qu'elle déchaîne le rire.³

[For me, the strongest [image] is one that presents the highest degree of arbitrariness . . . ; one that requires the longest time to translate into practical language, either because it contains an enormous dose of apparent contradiction, or because one of its terms is strangely hidden, or because it appears to unravel feebly after heralding itself as sensational . . . , or because it derives some ludicrous *formal* justification from itself, or because of its hallucinatory nature, or because it very naturally lays the mask of the concrete upon abstract things, or vice versa, or because it implies the negation of some elementary physical property, or because it unleashes laughter.]

Obviously, the formation of figures of speech or tropes is proscribed and, if it occurs, is accidental. Characterized by immediacy and incongruence, surrealist images bypass all willful intellectual controls. They are not subject to interpretation during their creation. Thereafter, interpretation (at least by their surrealist creator) is relevant only insofar as coincidence and happenstance may reveal their hitherto unforeseen significance. The poem « Tournesol » [Sunflower], written in 1923 but later revealed to have been premonitory, is a celebrated case in point (see first note to "Sunflower," p. 288). What I shall call the imagenic process of surrealism not only produces disparate and unanticipated images; it also works to verbalize the unconscious associations which occur in dreams, including those that reason interprets as contradictory. Image incompatibility betokens the disfranchisement of reason. Breton is keenly aware of Freud's discovery that, in dreams, the categories of contradiction and opposition are voided, that the unconscious is blind to negation, and that dreams evince a particular tendency to join opposites together into a unit or to represent them in a single object.[4] In the surrealist perspective, antinomies are never dissolved nor definitively re-solved; notwithstanding the tension of desire that propels them toward resolution, they are preserved as dynamic and symbiotic correlatives. Breton derived further corroboration of this view from another quarter:

Il va sans dire que ce « point, » en quoi sont appelées à se résoudre toutes les antinomies qui nous rongent et nous désespèrent . . . , ne saurait aucunement se situer sur le plan

mystique. Inutile d'insister sur ce que peut avoir d' « hégéli-
en » l'idée d'un tel dépassement de toutes les antinomies. C'est
incontestablement Hegel . . . qui m'a mis dans les conditions
voulues pour apercevoir ce point, pour tendre de toutes mes for-
ces vers lui et pour faire, de cette tension même, l'objet de ma
vie. . . . Où la dialectique hégélienne ne fonctionne pas, il n'y a
pas pour moi de pensée, pas d'espoir de vérité.[5]

[It goes without saying that the "point" at which all antino-
mies that rankle and distress us are destined to be resolved is
in no way to be found on a mystical level. There is no need to
stress how the idea of overcoming all antinomies is "Hegelian."
Unquestionably, it is Hegel . . . who enabled me to perceive
this point, to tend toward it with all my strength, and to make
of this very tension my life's goal. [. . .] Where the Hegelian
dialectic does not function, there is for me no thought, no hope
for truth.]

The anharmonic bias proclaimed by Breton and evident in his poetry
cannot be ascribed only to his tone deafness, admitted by him and con-
firmed by others; it is wholly consistent with his vision of man and the
world. The very word *harmony,* he wrote in 1922, is meaningless.[6] Pleasure
is conveyed through accident and surprise, whether discordant or other-
wise. « Je n'ai jamais éprouvé le plaisir intellectuel que sur le plan analo-
gique. Pour moi la seule *évidence* au monde est commandée par le rapport
spontané, extra-lucide, insolent qui s'établit, dans certaines conditions, entre
telle chose et telle autre, que le sens commun retiendrait de confronter. »[7] [I
have never experienced intellectual pleasure except on an analogical level.
For me, what is unmistakably *real* is determined by the spontaneous, clair-
voyant, insolent relation that, under certain conditions, connects one thing
with another, and that common sense would be loath to confront.]

Whereas the logical mode sets inflexible limits, the analogical mode
allows access to the realm of "absolute possibility."[8] The joy of analogical
discovery presupposes a constant receptivity or *disponibilité* to revelatory
signs and events, but also an eagerness to invite the occurrence of such
phenomena. All of Breton's writings express the anticipation of strange
but happy coincidences, the delight provoked by sudden, random revela-
tions born of objective chance *(le hasard objectif),* and the celebration of

serendipity. In one of his most important essays, first published in 1934 and later incorporated as the opening chapter of *L'Amour fou* [Mad Love] (1937), Breton describes "convulsive beauty," certainly one of the most significant concepts of modern art. Several of its key features may be summarized here.

Breton first posits a relationship between beauty and sexuality. Aesthetic emotion, whether induced by a natural spectacle or by a work of art, is signaled without warning by a feeling of inner disturbance *[un trouble]* or by a shudder *[un frisson]*. He adds: « Je n'ai jamais pu m'empêcher d'établir une relation entre cette sensation et celle du plaisir érotique et ne découvre entre elles que des différences de degré. »[9] [I could never avoid establishing a relation between such a sensation and that of erotic pleasure, and can only discover differences of degree between them.] The experience of beauty, animate or inanimate, is thus the fulfillment of desire, of a desire sought and sustained by cultivating "states of perfect receptivity." Aesthetic emotion is of course always characterized by unpredictability and *dépaysement*.

Breton then goes on to define convulsive beauty not as motion proper, but as « l'expiration exacte de ce mouvement » [the very moment at which movement stops], that is, motion in suspension or in repose. Among several examples adduced to illustrate the idea of convulsive beauty, the most striking is that of a high-speed locomotive abandoned for many years in a virgin forest and overwhelmed by an unruly wilderness, an image found in the poem « Facteur Cheval » [Postman Cheval] in *Le Revolver à cheveux blancs:*

Tu t'en souviens tu te levais alors tu descendais du train
Sans un regard pour la locomotive en proie aux immenses
    racines barométriques
Qui se plaint dans la forêt vierge de toutes ses chaudières
    meurtries
Ses cheminées fumant de jacinthes et mue par des serpents
    bleus

[You remember you would arise then you would step off the
    train
Without a glance at the locomotive preyed upon by immense
    barometric roots
That cries out dolefully in the virgin forest with all of its
    mauled boilers
Its stacks puffing hyacinths and propelled by blue serpents]

The image vividly symbolizes the victory of the unconscious over the conscious. The locomotive, as a male symbol, has penetrated the virgin forest, identified with the female principle, and has been absorbed by it. A complex artifact constructed by human ingenuity as a powerful vehicle for the fulfillment of human imagination and desire is assimilated by the raw power of nature.

Breton cites other illustrations of convulsive beauty drawn from the range of natural phenomena: stalagmites, coral, and crystal. Each constitutes, in the realm of nature, « le merveilleux précipité du désir »[10] [the marvelous precipitate of desire]. Crystal, a particularly frequent image in Breton, defined by him as the perfect expression of spontaneous action and creation. The hardness and transparency of crystal correspond to that "moment where the mobile and unceasing activity of magnetism achieves complete repose," a definition borrowed from Hegel and quoted by Breton in a letter written two years earlier.[11] Coral is an example of natural ambiguity and contiguity, the passing of the animate into the inanimate being termed by Breton « tout ce qu'il y a de subtil au monde, tout ce à quoi la connaissance n'accède que lourde-ment par degrés »[12] [everything that is subtle in the world, everything that knowledge arrives at but ponderously and by degrees].

The four examples of convulsive beauty cited by Breton share certain characteristics. The locomotive trapped in the virgin forest, stalagmites, crystal, and coral—all embody immobilized, frozen motion, motion in seeming suspension, yet ever potential and virtual, a *stasis* subject to imperceptible change. Paradox is an intrinsic element of beauty: arrested motion is susceptible of ulterior development; time is frozen, yet the process of creation, of accretion, and of subsidence is ever implied. Convulsive beauty arises from an exquisite balance between action and inertia, perpetuated by the hidden laws of spontaneity and chance. Breton has clearly refined in this essay his previous definition, stated in *Nadja* (1928), of convulsive beauty as « ni dynamique, ni statique » [neither dynamic, nor static].

Finally, convulsiveness is not an inherent quality of things, but an impregnation brought about by external influences, the result of a dialectical process. The locomotive, stalagmites, crystal, and coral are nothing without the forest, cave, grotto, and ocean in which they are so to speak consummated. The reader cannot but notice that the latter are all feminine symbols, and the former, masculine. Their interplay yields yet another seeming paradox, namely that the feminine principle fecundates the masculine, not vice versa. That Animus fulfills its potential only when it is nurtured by Anima[13] is a constant in the writings of Breton, who elsewhere approvingly cites Goethe's last thought that "the Eternal Feminine is in truth the keystone of the edifice," and the observation by the German physicist and theosophist J. W Ritter (1776–1810) that "man, stranger on earth, is acclimatized here below by woman alone."[14] To which Breton adds in conclusion: « C'est pourquoi l'amour et les femmes sont la plus claire solution de toutes les énigmes. » [That is why love and women are the clearest solution to all enigmas.] Such is, of course, the message later developed in *Arcane 17* (1944) and resumed in *Du Surréalisme en ses œuvres vives* [Of Surrealism in Its Living Works] (1953). The reader will perhaps remember that Breton establishes a link between convulsive beauty and erotic pleasure at the beginning of his essay. The very image of convulsiveness is of course sexual. That it constitutes a metaphor for the consummation of desire and for orgasmic fulfillment is implicit in Breton's writings:

> Et nous prenions les attitudes de ton plaisir
> Immobiles sous nos paupières pour toujours comme la femme
>   aime voir l'homme
> Après avoir fait l'amour

> [And we would take on the configurations of your pleasure
> Motionless beneath our eyelids forever as a woman loves to see
>   a man
> After making love]
>   (« Facteur Cheval »)

> Squales dont le ventre blanc s'incorpore le dernier frisson des
>   draps
> A l'heure de l'amour et des paupières bleues

> [Sharks' white bellies absorb the sheets' last quiver
> At the hour of love and of blue eyelids]
>   (« Vigilance, » from *Le Revolver à cheveux blancs*)

> Tu avais gravé les signes infaillibles
> De mon enchantement

Au moyen d'un poignard dont le manche de corail bifurque à
   l'infini
Pour que ton sang et le mien
N'en fassent qu'un

[You had etched the unfailing signs
Of my enchantment
By means of a dagger whose coral handle bifurcates to infinity
So that your blood and mine
Make but one]

(« Il allait être cinq heures du matin »
[It was about to be five in the morning],
from L'Air de l'eau)

Ouf le basilic est passé tout près sans me voir
Qu'il revienne je tiens braqué sur lui le miroir
Où est faite pour se consommer la jouissance humaine
   imprescriptible
Dans une convulsion que termine un éclaboussement de
   plumes dorées

[Whew the basilisk passed close by without seeing me
Just let him come back I've got my mirror trained on him
Unprescribable human joy is made there to be consummated
In a convulsion ended by a splash of gilded feathers]

(Fata Morgana)

   Although it might be concluded from the examples cited by Breton in
his essay that convulsiveness is primarily associated with material, real-life
objects, there is no doubt that the most striking literary images also sug-
gest it. In this regard, Breton singles out Rimbaud and Lautréamont as
the paramount originators of modern poetry. The impression of *dépayse-
ment* produced by their imagery is directly attributable to the hallucinatory
combination of disparate and incongruous elements. Lautréamont's now
famous similes, writes Breton, "constituent le manifeste même de la poésie
convulsive"[15] [constitute the very manifesto of convulsive poetry]. Witness
these lines:

Le vautour des agneaux, beau comme la loi de l'arrêt de développement de la poitrine chez les adultes dont la propension à la croissance n'est pas en rapport avec la quantité de molécules que leur organisme s'assimile, se perdit dans les hautes couches de l'atmosphère.[16]

[The lamb vulture, as lovely as the law of arrested development of the chest in adults whose propensity to grow bears no relation to the quantity of molecules that their organism assimilates, vanished into the upper layers of the atmosphere.]

Or again, referring to an adolescent:

II est beau comme la rétractilité des serres des oiseaux rapaces; ou encore, comme l'incertitude des mouvements circulaires dans les plaies des parties molles de la région cervicale postérieure; ou plutôt, comme ce piège à rats perpétuel, toujours retendu par l'animal pris, qui peut prendre seul des rongeurs indéfiniment, et fonctionner même caché sous la paille; et surtout, comme la rencontre fortuite sur une table de dissection d'une machine à coudre et d'un parapluie![17]

[He is as lovely as the retractility of the claws of birds of prey; or yet again, as the uncertainty of circular motion in the sores of the soft parts of the brain's posterior area; or rather, as a perpetual rat trap, ever reset by the captured animal, capable by itself of indefinitely trapping rodents and of functioning even when hidden under straw; and especially, as the chance encounter on a dissecting table of a sewing machine and an umbrella!]

The genesis of poetic imagery and its kinship with the oneiric (or at least unconscious) process is a matter that fascinated the surrealists, who, least of all Breton, never claimed to have found the key to its mystery. Whether word-images translate the imagenic chemistry of the unconscious, or whether dreams are themselves a visual translation of verbal elements, is of course a chicken-or-the-egg dilemma that warrants no discussion here. Like the mystery of love itself, it remains, to use Breton's admirable phrase, an « infracassable noyau de *nuit* »[18] [unshatterable kernel of *night*]. Yet the means by which Breton sought to express the "subliminal message"[19] is one of the most significant—if admittedly imperfect—contributions of surrealism to modern writing. Beginning in 1919, Breton's attention had been drawn to the occurrence of sentence fragments in his mind as he approached somnolence. These sentences had struck him as revealing an unexpectedly rich imagery within normal syntactical patterns. Initially, he felt impelled to consign the most remarkable of these involuntary images to memory. Only later did it occur to him and to Philippe Soupault that similar imagenic states could be reconstituted voluntarily. The outcome was the first "automatic" text, *Les Champs magnétiques* [Magnetic Fields], a series of prose poems written by Breton and Soupault in eight feverish days and published in 1919–1920. The authors had induced what might be termed self-hypnotic trances, thus enormously enhancing their receptivity to the subliminal messages dictated by their inner voices. In the process, they in effect became the passive scribes of their unconscious. The hallucinogenic impact of such sessions, while literarily fruitful, nonetheless gave Breton pause. An inherent peril lay in the impression that such images could make upon the conscious mind, namely an increasing inability to retain a sense of reality. In a later (1930) commentary on the production of *Les Champs magnétiques,*[20] Breton acknowledged that he had felt at times possessed by the mental images that had emerged from such hypnotic trances, and that madness or even suicide lurked just around the corner. Referring to the image « pneus pattes de velours » [tires velvet paws] in the third poem, "Eclipses," Breton indicated that it had caused him to fancy himself pursued by cats one afternoon when crossing the Place de l'Etoile. Such personal experiences were confirmed by the alarming turn taken during a number of collective sessions devoted to dream narration and automatic writing in 1922. The spectre of violent and self-destructive behavior on the part of the participants led Breton to terminate these sessions, most memorable for the extraordinary streams of unconsciousness that gushed forth from the mouth and pen of Robert Desnos. The pitfalls of automatic writing quickly became evident. The experiment consisted in attempting to capture the continuum of involuntary verbal representation and to set it down in writing without bringing to bear any kind of qualitative judgment. As Breton explained in a revealing essay written in 1933, the intended result was, of course, to « puiser aveuglément dans le trésor subjectif pour la seule tentation de jeter de-ci de-là sur le sable une poignée d'algues écumeuses et d'émeraudes »[21] [to dip blindly into the subjective treasure simply from a temptation to cast here and there upon the sand a handful of emeralds and foam-laden seaweed].

Such remarks on the nature of verbal inspiration in automatic writing are noteworthy for the light they shed on the surrealist (or at least Bretonian) imagenic process. A critical distinction is established between "verbo-auditory" images and strictly visual images; that is, between images resulting from the spontaneous emergence of words and those that occur without the accompaniment of words in the imagination alone. Purely visual images are deemed to be highly disruptive of the verbal "murmur," less continuous, and much more difficult to capture. In the final analysis, he says,

> je tiens . . . les inspirations verbales pour infiniment plus riches de sens visuel . . . que les images visuelles proprement dites. De là la protestation que je n'ai jamais cessé d'élever contre le prétendu pouvoir « visionnaire » du poète. Non, Lautréamont, Rimbaud n'ont pas vu, n'ont pas joui *a priori* de ce qu'ils décrivaient . . . . L'« illumination » vient *ensuite*.[22]

> [I hold . . . verbal inspiration to be infinitely richer in visual meaning . . . than visual proper. That is why I have never ceased to raise my voice in protest against the alleged "visionary" power of poets. No, Lautréamont, Rimbaud did not see, did not enjoy *a priori* what they were describing. . . . "Illumination" comes *afterward*.]

In sum, words do not attempt to describe visual images; words create them. Words make love;[23] images are born from their latent sympathies and magnetic properties. Like a living organism, language has its own biochemistry, its own metabolism. In reacting to and with each other, words arouse their many reciprocal latencies and expose their hidden complicity.[24] Listening to the words spoken within and transcribing them brought to Breton intense feelings of deliverance and euphoria. The writer's joy is that of being the unwitting but willing agent of happy coincidences, of discovering the marvelous not in oneself but in the images created by the random, unforeseen concatenation of words within orthodox, although often disconcerting, syntactical structures. The latter point is an important, if perhaps surprising one, at least at first glance. In surrealism, linguistic coherence is preserved, for it is not the syntactical or lexical corpus of language that is challenged. Language is, after all, a legacy of the collective unconscious, the result of a complex, age-old, ongoing dialectical process. Automatic writing thus never threatened to disrupt or disregard the laws of language. In 1924, Breton stated: « Rien ne sert de modifier [les mots] puisque, tels qu'ils sont, ils répondent avec cette promptitude à notre appel. . . . Je sais le sens de tous mes mots et j'observe *naturellement* la syntaxe . . . qui n'est pas, comme le croient certains sots, une discipline. »[25] [There is no need to modify [words] since, just as they are, they answer our call with such promptness. . . I know the meaning of all my words and *naturally* conform to syntax . . . which is not, as some fools believe, a discipline.] Thirty years later, Breton again observed in reference to automatic writing, « L'expérience a montré qu'y passaient fort peu de néologismes et qu'il n'entraînait ni démembrement syntactique ni désintégration du vocabulaire. »[26] [Experience has shown that very few neologisms found their way into it, and that it entailed neither syntactical dismemberment nor the disintegration of vocabulary.]

Language affects, and is affected by, its practitioners. It must be allowed to function, to signify its own desires. T. S. Eliot's observation that the modern poet's job is "to force, to dislocate if necessary, language into his meaning,"[27] if subjected to surrealist scrutiny, is susceptible to some dislocation of its own: in a surrealist image, it is language itself that forces and dislocates meaning. Breton's position with regard to the meaning of images is stated in a pithy comment inserted in the « Introduction au Discours sur le peu de réalité » [Introduction to the Discourse on the Dearth of Reality], written in 1924, where he quotes a critic who attempted to explain images in the poetry of Saint-Pol-Roux (1861–1941), greatly admired by the surrealists as a precursor and one of theirs:

> *Lendemain de chenille en tenue de bal* veut dire: papillon.
> *Mamelle de cristal* veut dire: une carafe.[28]

> [*Morrow of a caterpillar in evening dress* means: butterfly.
> *Breast of crystal* means: a decanter.]

Breton retorted:

Non, monsieur, *ne veut pas dire.* Rentrez votre papillon dans votre carafe. Ce que Saint-Pol-Roux a voulu dire, soyez certain qu'il l'a dit.[29]

[No, sir, *does not mean.* Put your butterfly back into your decanter. What Saint-Pol-Roux meant to say, you can be sure he said.]

Surrealist imagery draws its meaning not from interpretation or explanation but from the raw immediacy of its illuminative power. Its success is measured by the degree of *dépaysement* it generates. Breton cites the following image produced by automatic writing as an example among others of hallucinatory imagery:

Sur le pont la rosée à tête de chatte se berçait[30]

[On the bridge the pussy-headed dew was swaying to and fro]

Analysis becomes pertinent only after it has been preceded by spontaneous delight. Knowledge and understanding are ancillary. « Au départ, il ne s'agit pas de comprendre mais *d'aimer.* . . . Les lacunes de compréhension sont . . . sans importance, à supposer même qu'elles ne soient pas les bienvenues pour que s'y épanchent sans obstacle les rayons du cœur, comme les clairières dans les bois. »[31] [At the outset, it is only *liking,* not understanding, that matters. . . . Gaps in understanding . . . are not only unimportant, they are perhaps even welcome, like clearings in the woods, the better to allow the heart's rays to stream out without obstacle.] The unlit shadows, he concludes, should remain obscure, which is the very condition of enchantment.

The practice of automatic writing did not yield uniformly "successful" results. Breton, who was the first to acknowledge the occurrence of many a slip twixt the cup, the lip, and the pen, never claimed any surrealist text to be a perfect example of verbal automatism. A minimal degree of authorial guidance subsists, particularly « dans le sens de l'*arrangement en poème,* »[32] that is, in the distribution of sentences into lines of poetry. Among the texts presented in this anthology, automatism is most evident in the poems of *Clair de terre* [Earthlight] (1923) and *Poisson soluble* [Soluble Fish] (1924). Thereafter, though its flux never ceases to irrigate Breton's poetry, it becomes less intensive, more intermittent. The imagery nonetheless continues to reflect the dictation of an inexhaustible inner voice. The reader is, of course, not aware of the extent of authorial intervention, if any. As for the first collection, *Mont de piété* [Pawnshop] (1919), it belongs to an entirely different phase in Breton's development. Its poems are notable for a high incidence of intertextuality; a number of them include more or less concealed quotations from, or oblique references to, works by other writers (Rimbaud, Mallarmé, Lautréamont, Jarry, Apollinaire, Gide, Valéry). These references are stubbornly, indeed gleefully, cryptic. Their hermeticism is deliberate and their composition exemplifies the most aggressive kind of deconstruction, achieved by means of discontinuity, ellipsis, disharmony, and ambiguity. Their purpose was frankly terroristic, in the manner of Dada. Breton sought to gut the "pohème" from the inside, thus contributing to the death of *ancien régime* art and literature. In this regard, the turn to automatism was a natural reaction against the highly conscious and intellectual tenor of his first poems. The last major collection of poems, *Constellations* (1959), written as an accompaniment to a series of similarly entitled gouaches by Joan Miró), attests impressively to the felicitous balance between automatism and arrangement that Breton could achieve in his later poetry. These prose poems offer a brilliant array of surrealist images set like jewels in a highly condensed, magnetically charged, often idiosyncratic (but never aberrant) prose.

The reading of any poetic text of Breton is likely to elicit a number of simultaneous, often conflicting reactions. A not inconsiderable effort is required to adjust to a style characterized by the absence of normal logical or rhetorical props, and tending toward syntactical patterns of unusual complexity. The impression of *dépaysement* arises not only from the imagery; it is a function of the very texture of surrealist discourse. It has been noted that in yielding to automatism, Breton's rapid writing mirrors the autistic process, marked by withdrawal into extreme fantasy.[33] Autism expresses itself through undirected thought and day-dreaming, both of which surrealism sought to convey verbally. Besides the imagery, the single feature of Breton's style that most appreciably contributes to its power of disconcertion is a highly disjunctive, centrifugal syntax. Beneath the often seemingly hypotactic arrangement of his discourse, the syntagmatic linkage is in fact very loose. For example, Breton's fondness for relative and subordinate clauses, most notable after 1932, is deceptive in that the effective function of such relative pronouns as *qui, que, dont,* etc., is less to subordinate than to concatenate. The result of such *phrases à tiroirs,* or embedded clauses, is on the one hand to diffract, on the other to accomplish a particular kind of continuum, the continuum of undirected discourse. In the end, the hypotactic trappings are subverted, the discourse verges on parataxis:

> Tourbillon qui emporte l'esprit qui me regagne à l'illusion
>   enfantine
> Que tout est là pour quelque chose qui me concerne

> [Whirlwind that sweeps away the mind that wins me back to
>   the childlike illusion
> That all is there for something that affects me]
>   (*Fata Morgana*)

> Leur rêverie se veloute de la chair d'une pensée proportionnée aux dimensions de l'œil cyclopéen qu'ouvrent les lacs et dont la fixité fascina qui devait se faire le terrible héraut du Retour Eternel.

> [Their reverie softens like the velvety flesh of a thought pro-
> -portioned to the dimensions of the cyclopean eye that the lakes open and whose spellbinding steady stare was to become the terrible harbinger of the Eternal Return.]
>   (« Femmes au bord d'un lac . . . »
>   *Constellations,* [Women by the shore of a lake . . .])

Other features that contribute to the exploded syntax of automatic or semiautomatic writing can be discerned in the examples given below, grouped in five categories:

1. Interruption and resumption—resolution of the sentence is deferred by the insertion of one or more syntactically unrelated phrases (asides, phrases in apposition, digressions):

> Pfuût houch le coup de revolver le sang qui saute lestement les
>   marches vertes
> Pas assez vite pour que l'homme [→]
> Son signalement 1 m. 65 la concierge n'a pas osé arrêter ce visiteur
>   inhabituel mais poli
> Il était d'autre part très bien de sa personne

[→] Ne s'éloigne en allumant une cigarette
Plus douce que la douleur d'aimer et d'être aimé

[Pfft whoosh the pistol shot blood leaping nimbly down the green
steps
Not fast enough to prevent the man [→]
His description 1.65 meters tall the concierge didn't dare stop this
unusual but polite visitor
Besides he cut a very dashing figure
[→] From moving away lighting a cigarette
Sweeter than the pain of loving and being loved]
(« Sans connaissance » [Unconscious],
in *Le Revolver à cheveux blancs*)

2. Abrupt shifts in registers of language—from formal or lyrical to famil-
iar or conversational, or vice versa:

Ménisques adorable rideau de tangence quand la vie n'est plus
qu'une aigrette qui boit
Et dis-toi qu'aussi bien je ne te verrai plus

[Meniscuses lovely curtain of tangency when life is but a drink-
ing egret
And you might as well know that besides I shall not see you any
more]
(« Frôleuse » [Flirt], in *1940–1943*)

3. Ambiguity and disjunction by syntactical rearrangement, scrambling,
or inversion—syntagmatic components are distributed or juxtaposed with-
out logical or rhetorical linearity:

Un jour un nouveau jour cela me fait penser à un objet que garde
mon ami Wolfgang Paalen
D'une corde déjà grise tous les modèles de nœuds réunis sur une
planchette
Je ne sais pourquoi il déborde tant le souci didactique qui a présidé
à sa construction sans doute pour une école de marins

Bien que l'ingéniosité de l'homme donne ici sa fleur que nimbe
   la nuée des petits singes aux yeux pensifs
En vérité aucune page des livres même virant au pain bis n'at-
   teint à cette vertu conjuratoire rien ne m'est si propice
Un nouvel amour et que d'autres tant pis se bornent à adorer

[One day a new day that makes me think of an object kept by
   my friend Wolfgang Paalen
From a rope already grey all the kinds of knots assembled on a
   plank
I don't know why it goes beyond far beyond the didactic concern
   that guided its construction doubtless for a seafarers' school
Although human cleverness here brings forth its full flower
   edged with a bright cloud of tiny monkeys with thoughtful
   eyes
Really not one page of the books even turning to brown bread
   reaches this exorcising power nothing is so propitious to me
A new love and too bad may others confine themselves to
   adoring]

(Fata Morgana)

The most extreme case of scrambling and inversion is to be found in a
prose poem from *Constellations*, « Femme à la blonde aisselle . . ." » [Woman
with blond armpit . . .].

4. Abrupt shifts by ellipsis or grammatical shortcutting:

Il y a ce que je connais bien ce que je connais si peu que prête-
   moi tes serres vieux délire

[There is what I know well what I know so little that lend me
   your claws old delirium]

(« Nœud des miroirs » [Knot of Mirrors], in
Le Revolver à cheveux blancs)

Mais les gens sont si bien en train de se noyer
   Que ne leur demandez pas de saisir la perche

[But people are so well on the way to drowning themselves
That don't ask them to grab the pole being held out for them]
(Fata Morgana)

5. Hinge words—words straddling two otherwise unrelated words or phrases, thereby conjoining them into a word play:

Cet instant fait dérailler le train rond des pendules

[That instant derails the clocks' round train]
(« Sans connaissance »)

where *train* refers both to a vehicle and to the pace of a clock.

Another distinctive feature of Breton's style commands attention: the frequent use of certain prepositions, chiefly *à* and *de*, notable for their versatility. Favored by Breton for their agglutinative virtue, they are one of the most common coordinating units of his imagery. In this respect, Breton's practice parallels that of Raymond Roussel (1877–1933), who raised the use of *à* to the status of a literary device, thereby gaining possession of a key to the imagination: « Je choisissais un mot, puis le reliais à un autre par la préposition à. » [I would choose a word, then link it to another by the preposition à.] Quoting Roussel's recipe, Breton added: « La préposition en question apparaît bien, en effet, poétiquement, comme le véhicule de beaucoup le plus rapide et le plus sûr de l'image. J'ajouterai qu'il suffit de relier ainsi *n'importe quel* substantif à *n'importe quel* autre pour qu'un monde de représentations nouvelles surgisse aussitôt. »[34] [The preposition referred to does indeed appear, poetically, to be by far the swiftest and surest vehicle of images. I might add that linking *any* substantive to *any* other is sufficient to make a world of new representations emerge at once.] Such prepositions as *à* and *de* in effect serve a purpose similar to that of relative pronouns or simple coordinating conjunctions like *et* and *ou*. The most striking example is found in the aptly titled *L'Union libre* [Free Union], perhaps Breton's best-known poem, whose 60 lines emblazoning the female body are constructed entirely by means of images introduced by à (52 times) and fused by *de* (108 times), with a scattering of other prepositions *(dans, sur, sous, entre, pour)*. The poem is a dazzling litany of surrealist love images connected by repetition alone, without the aid of conjunctions or main-clause verbs:

Ma femme à la chevelure de feu de bois
Aux pensées d'éclairs de chaleur
A la taille de sablier
Ma femme à la taille de loutre entre les dents du tigre
Ma femme à la bouche de cocarde et de bouquet d'étoiles de
    dernière grandeur
Aux dents d'empreintes de souris blanche sur la terre blanche A
    la langue d'ambre et de verre frottés
Ma femme à la langue d'hostie poignardée
A la langue de poupée qui ouvre et ferme les yeux
A la langue de pierre incroyable

[My love whose hair is woodfire
Her thoughts heat lightning
Her hourglass waist
An otter in the tiger's jaws my love
Her mouth a rosette bouquet of stars of the highest magnitude
The footprints of white mice on the white earth her teeth
Her tongue rubbed amber and glass
My love her tongue a sacred host stabbed through
Her tongue a doll whose eyes close and open
Her tongue an incredible stone]

In the foregoing text, *à* serves to characterize by association. In other
instances, it can denote purpose or consequence:

La peur à oublier ses doigts dans un livre pour ne plus toucher
A fermer ses yeux dans le sillage du premier venu pour éperdu-
    ment le fuir

[Such fear as to forget one's fingers in a book in order to touch
    no more
As to shut one's eyes in the wake of a chance encounter in order
    to flee desperately from that person]
                         (« Sans connaissance »)

Du dehors l'air est à se refroidir

[From outside the air is fit to cool one down]
   (« Le puits enchanté » [The Enchanted Well], in *1935–1940*)

. . . et de l'eau encore s'égoutte à l'accorder des hauts instruments
   de cuivre vert.
[. . . and water again is dripping to attune it from the lofty in-
   struments of green copper.]
                              (« La Lanterne sourde » [The Dark Lantern],
                                         in *Des Epingles tremblantes*)

Subordinating conjunctions are predictably rare, and causal conjunctions
simply absent, causality being completely alien to surrealist discourse:

Aussi vrai que le mot le plus haïssable me paraît être le mot
donc . . . , j'aime éperdûment tout ce qui, rompant d'aventure le
fil de la pensée discursive, part soudain en fusée illuminant une
vie de relations autrement féconde . . . [35]

[Just as the most hateful word seems to me to be the word *there-*
fore . . . , I passionately love everything that, by chance breaking
the thread of discursive thought, suddenly flares up and illumi-
nates a far more fruitful life of relationships . . .]

Demonstrative adjectives play as deceptive and paradoxical a role as do
relative pronouns: rather than demonstrate or serve as referents, they beto-
ken psychological immediacy and act as intensifiers:

Et soudain ce froissement de fleurs et d'aiguilles de glace
Ces sourcils verts ce balancier d'étoile filante

[And suddenly this ruffling of flowers and ice needles
These green eyebrows this balancing-pole of a shooting star]

                              (« Il allait être cinq heures du matin »)

A similar effect is achieved by the more ordinary means of the definite article, of which there is an overwhelming preponderance in Breton's poetic discourse.

The syntactical and lexical plays so consistently present in Breton's writings reflect his fascination with chance, manifest not only in automatic writing but also in the extensive practice of graphic or verbal games and riddles engaged in by all the surrealists. The success of such ludic activity was of course measured in terms not of rivalry but of surprise. In the surrealist perspective, games were experiments in chance, not contests. They were intended to elicit a discovery, not a solution. Language itself is a ludic phenomenon, for it is the ad-venture of words, their chance encounter and association, that reveals and delights. Word-plays issuing from the "love-making" of words are constantly encountered in all of Breton's poetry, the attendant impression generated being one of ambiguity and *dépaysement*. Surrealist literary creation does not enact aesthetic concerns, but an adventuresome way of life, a poethics reflecting and affecting all aspects of human existence.

Breton's extraordinary lexicon merits some commentary here. The very high incidence of botanical, zoological, entomological, ornithological, and ichthyological terms is striking indeed. Use of recondite vocabulary becomes extensive in the later works, culminating in the quasi-baroque, *précieux* lexical (and syntactical) richness of *Constellations*. Breton's explanation of his use of zoological terminology is interesting: « . . . le bestiaire surréaliste, sur toutes les autres espèces, accorde la prééminence à des types hors série, d'aspect aberrant ou fin de règne comme l'ornithorynque, la mante religieuse ou le tamanoir »[36] [. . . the surrealist bestiary gives preeminence above all species to out-of-the-ordinary types, aberrant or end-of-a-line in aspect, like the duck-billed platypus, the praying mantis, or the great anteater]. A revealing statement indeed, summing up as it does what earlier observations have, I hope, served to show—namely that what characterizes Breton's poetry and the surrealist vision is the primary role of the irregular and the anomalous, seen as purveyors of the marvelous within an essentially naturalistic universe. Breton's writings all attest to the profound respect in which he held the world of nature. The animal, vegetable, and mineral kingdoms are repositories of the marvelous, the images drawn from them being always those of a poet:

Aux yeux de niveau d'eau de niveau d'air de terre et de feu

[Eyes of water level earth and air and fire]

(*L'Union libre*)

Breton's poetry challenges the reader to perform an exacting task. Understanding surrealist discourse does not come easily, even to the initiated, and is often intermittent at best. Its linguistic and cultural content is so extensive, allusive, and elusive as to become hermetic. But that is, so to speak, the very nature of the beast. For the marvelous and the surreal are seldom immediately perceived, let alone understood. It is their irruption into our consciousness, however fleeting, however flickering, that matters:

Juste ce qu'il faut pour que transparaisse . . . Le message in-
déchiffrable capital

[Just enough to make the paramount undecipherable message
Show through . . .]

(« A ta place . . . » [If I were you . . .],
in *L'Air de l'eau*)

POEMS OF ANDRÉ BRETON
A Bilingual Anthology

▲

Signature of André Breton at conclusion of his letter to Joe Bousquet, July 10, 1930. Reproduced by permission of the Humanities Research Center, The University of Texas at Austin.

From *Mont de piété* [Pawnshop]
1919

Age[1]

Aube, adieu! Je sors du bois hanté; j'affronte les routes, croix torrides. Un feuillage bénissant me perd. L'août est sans brèches comme une meule.[2]

Retiens la vue panoramique, hume l'espace et dévide machinalement les fumées.

Je vais m'élire une enceinte précaire: on enjambera s'il faut le buis. La province aux bégonias chauffés caquète, range. Que gentiment s'ameutent les griffons au volant frisé des jupes!

Où la chercher, depuis les fontaines? A tort je me fie à son collier de bulles . . .

Yeux devant les pois de senteur.

*

Chemises caillées sur la chaise. Un chapeau de soie inaugure de reflets ma poursuite. Homme . . . Une glace te venge et vaincu me traite en habit ôté. L'instant revient patiner la chair.

Maisons, je m'affranchis de parois sèches. On secoue![3] Un lit tendre est plaisanté de couronnes.[4]

Atteins la poésie accablante des paliers.

19 février 1916.

Age[I]

Dawn, farewell! I emerge from the haunted wood, brave the highways, torrid crosses. An ordaining foliage leads me astray. August is as free of fissures as a millstone.[2]

Cling to the panoramic view, sniff the space and reel off the smoke mechanically.

I shall choose for myself a precarious enclosure: We will jump the hedge if we must. The provinces full of heated begonias are chattering, tidying things up. How nicely the griffons troop around the ruffled flying of skirts!

Where to look after the fountains? I'm wrong to put my faith in her necklace of bubbles . . . .

Eyes before sweetpeas.

*

Shirts clotted on the chair. A silk top hat confers reflections upon my chase. Man . . . A mirror avenges you and, vanquished, treats me like a costume laid aside. The moment returns to lay its patina upon the flesh.

Houses, I free myself from dry walls. Somebody's shaking![3] A tender bed is teased with wreaths.[4]

Attain the overpowering poetry of stair landings.

February 19, 1916

(MAC)

Pour Lafcadio[1]

L'avenue   en même temps   le Gulf Stream
MAM VIVier[2]

Ma maîtresse[3]

    prend en bonne part
5   son diminutif Les amis
    sont à l'aise
        On s'entend
    Greffier[4]
    parlez MA langue MAternelle
10 *Quel ennui l'heure du cher corps*
    corps accort[5]
    Jamais je ne gagnerai tant de guerres

    Des combattants
    qu'importe mes vers le lent train
15 l'entrain[6]
    Mieux vaut laisser dire
    qu'André Breton
    receveur de Contributions Indirectes[7]
    s'adonne au collage[8]
20 en attendant la retraite[9]

For Lafcadio[I]

The avenue   at the same time   the Gulf Stream
MA'AM VIVier[2]

My mistress[3]
approves of
5 her nickname My friends
are at ease
      We get along well
   Clerk[4]
speak MY MOther tongue
10 *What a bother the dear body's time*
winsome body[5]
    Never shall I win so many wars

Fighters
no matter my verses the slow train
15 unrestrained[6]
Better let it be said
that André Breton
collector of excise taxes[7]
indulges in collages[8]
20 while awaiting retirement[9]

(JPC)

Monsieur V

à Paul Valéry

A la place de l'étoile[1]
L'Arc de Triomphe
qui ne ressemble à un aimant que pour la forme
    argenterai-je
5   les jardins suspendus

    BERCEUSE
    L'enfant à la capote de rubans
    L'enfant que chatouille la mer[2]
En grandissant
10 il se regarde dans une coquille nacrée
    l'iris de son œil est l'étoile dont je parlais

    MARCHE[3]
    Pierre ou Paul[4]
15 Il s'apprête à tirer les rois[5]
    aujourd'hui comme ailleurs
ses égaux
    Rêve de révolutions

    On ne saurait décrire en art
20 L'engin à prendre le renard bleu

Monsieur V

for Paul Valéry

Instead of a star [1]
The Arch of Triumph
which resembles a magnet by its shape only
shall I besilver
5   the hanging gardens

LULLABY
The child with the ribbon bonnet
The child tickled by the sea [2]
While growing
10   he looks at himself in a pearly shell
the iris of his eye is the star of
which I spoke

MARCH [3]
Peter or Paul [4]
15   He gets ready to draw a pair of kings [5]
today as elsewhere
his equals
A dream of revolutions

In art one can hardly describe
20   The device for catching the blue fox

(JPC)

Une Maison peu solide[1]

LE GARDIEN DES TRAVAUX
EST VICTIME DE SON DEVOUEMENT

Depuis longtemps le mode de construction d'un immeuble situé rue des Martyrs était jugé déraisonnable par les gens du quartier. Rien n'apparaissait encore de la toiture que déjà les peintres et les tapissiers entreprenaient de décorer les appartements. De nouveaux échafaudages étayaient tous les jours la façade chancelante, au grand trouble des passants que le gardien des travaux rassurait. Hélas! celui-ci devait payer son optimisme de la vie puisqu'hier, à midi trente, alors que les ouvriers étaient allés déjeuner, la bâtisse s'effondrait, l'ensevelissant sous ses décombres.

Un enfant, trouvé évanoui sur les lieux du sinistre, ne fut pas long à reprendre connaissance. C'est le jeune Lespoir,[2] 7 ans, que l'on reconduisit bien vite à ses parents. Il avait eu plus de peur que de mal. Il commença par réclamer la *trottinette* sur laquelle il s'était élancé du haut de la rue. Le garçonnet raconte qu'un homme avec un bâton s'étant précipité vers lui en criant « Gare! » il avait voulu s'enfuir. C'est tout ce dont il se souvient. On sait le reste. Son sauveur, bien connu de l'entourage sous le nom de Guillaume Apollinaire,[3] pouvait avoir une soixantaine d'années. Il avait gagné la médaille du travail et ses compagnons l'estimaient.

Quand pourrons-nous donner la clé de ce mystère? On recherche, en vain jusqu'à présent, l'entrepreneur et l'architecte de la maison penchée. L'émotion est considérable.

An Unsteady House[I]

SECURITY GUARD
IS VICTIM OF DEVOTION

For a long time the method followed in constructing a building on the rue des Martyrs had been judged unreasonable by the local inhabitants. The roofing had not even been installed, yet the painters and interior designers were already decorating the apartments. New scaffolding was being added daily to brace the tottering façade, causing great concern among passersby whom the security guard kept reassuring. Alas, he was destined to pay for his optimism with his life, for yesterday at twelve-thirty, while the workers were out to lunch, the building came crashing down, burying him under its rubble.

A child who was found unconscious on the scene of the tragedy soon regained his senses. Seven-year-old Lespoir[2] was quickly driven home to his parents. He had been more frightened than harmed. He promptly called for his *scooter* on which he had charged down the street. The boy reports that he attempted to flee from a man with a stick who rushed toward him crying "Watch it!" He remembers nothing else. The rest is common knowledge. His rescuer, well-known in the neighborhood as Guillaume Apollinaire,[3] was thought to be in his sixties. He had won the labor medal and was held in high regard by his companions.

When shall we be able to reveal the key to this mystery? The contractor and the architect of the leaning house are being sought, thus far in vain. Feelings are running high.

(JPC)

Le Corset Mystère

Mes belles lectrices,

à force d'en voir **de toutes les couleurs**
Cartes splendides, *à effets de lumière,* Venise
Autrefois les meubles de ma chambre étaient fixés solidement aux murs
et je me faisais attacher pour écrire:
5   **J'ai le pied marin**

nous adhérons à une sorte de **Touring Club** sentimental

UN CHÂTEAU À LA PLACE DE LA TÊTE
C'est aussi le **Bazar de la Charité**

10   Jeux très amusants pour tous âges;
                                    Jeux poétiques, etc.

Je tiens Paris comme—pour vous dévoiler l'avenir—votre main ouverte
la taille bien prise

The Mystery Corset

My lovely readers,

By seeing **in all colors**
Splendid postcards, *with lightning effects,* Venice
It used to be that my room's furnishings were solidly
5　　　　Fixed to the walls and I had to be strapped down to write
I'm a good sailor

We belong to a sort of sentimental **Touring Club**

A CHATEAU INSTEAD OF A HEAD
That's the **Charity Bazaar** *too*

10　　　Delightful games for all ages;
　　　　　　　　　　　　Poetic games, etc.

I hold Paris like—to unveil the future for you—your open hand
With a waist tightly bound

(MAC)

From *Clair de terre* [Earthlight]
1923

Amour parcheminé

Quand les fenêtres comme l'œil du chacal et le désir percent l'aurore, des treuils de soie me hissent sur les passerelles de la banlieue. J'appelle une fille qui rêve dans la maisonnette dorée; elle me rejoint sur les tas de mousse noire et m'offre ses lèvres qui sont des pierres au fond de la rivière rapide. Des pressentiments voilés descendent les marches des édifices. Le mieux est de fuir les grands cylindres de plume quand les chasseurs boitent dans les terres détrempées. Si l'on prend un bain dans la moire des rues, l'enfance revient au pays, levrette grise. L'homme cherche sa proie dans les airs et les fruits sèchent sur des claies de papier rose, à l'ombre des noms démesurés par l'oubli. Les joies et les peines se répandent dans la ville. L'or et l'eucalyptus, de même odeur, attaquent les rêves. Parmi les freins et les edelweiss sombres se reposent des formes souterraines semblables à des bouchons de parfumeurs.

Love in Parchment

When the windows like the jackal's eye and desire pierce the dawn, silken windlasses lift me up to suburban footbridges. I summon a girl who is dreaming in the little gilded house; she meets me on the piles of black moss and offers me her lips which are stones in the rapid river depths. Veiled forebodings descend the buildings' steps. The best thing is to flee from the great feather cylinders when the hunters limp into the sodden lands. If you take a bath in the watery patterns of the streets, childhood returns to the country like a greyhound. Man seeks his prey in the breezes and the fruits are drying on screens of pink paper, in the shadow of the names overgrown by forgetfulness. Joys and sorrows spread in the town. Gold and eucalyptus, similarly scented, attack dreams. Among the bridles and the dark edelweiss subterranean forms are resting like perfume bottle stoppers.

(MAC)

Cartes sur les dunes

à Giuseppe Ungaretti

L'horaire des fleurs creuses et des pommettes saillantes nous invite à quitter les salières volcaniques pour les baignoires d'oiseaux. Sur une serviette damée[1] rouge sont disposés les jours de l'année. L'air n'est plus si pur, la route n'est plus si large que le célèbre clairon.[2] Dans une valise peinte de gros vers[3] on emporte les soirs périssables qui sont la place des genoux sur un prie-Dieu. De petites bicyclettes côtelées tournent sur le comptoir. L'oreille des poissons, plus fourchue que le chèvrefeuille, écoute descendre les huiles bleues. Parmi les burnous éclatants dont la charge se perd dans les rideaux, je reconnais un homme issu de mon sang.

Cards on the Dunes

for Giuseppe Ungaretti

The schedule of hollow flowers and prominent cheekbones invites us to leave the volcanic salt-cellars for bird bathtubs. On a red-trumped[1] napkin the days of the year are arranged. The air is not as clear, the road no longer as wide as the famous bugle.[2] Inside a suitcase on which big worms[3] are painted, perishable evenings are carried away—they are the position of the knees on a prayer-stool. Small ribbed bicycles turn on the countertop. The ear of fishes, more forked than honeysuckle, listens to the descending blue oils. Among the dazzling burnooses that lose their charge in the curtains, I recognize a man begotten from my blood.

(JPC)

à Francis Picabia[1]

C'est aussi le bagne avec ses brèches blondes comme un livre sur les
    genoux d'une jeune fille
Tantôt il est fermé et crève de peine[2] future sur les remous d'une
    mer à pic
Un long silence a suivi ces meurtres
L'argent se dessèche sur les rochers
5   Puis sous une apparence de beauté ou de raison contre toute
    apparence aussi
Et les deux mains dans une seule palme
On voit le soir
Tomber collier de perles des monts
Sur l'esprit de ces peuplades tachetées règne un amour si plaintif
10   Que les devins se prennent à ricaner bien haut sur les ponts de fer
Les petites statues se donnent la main à travers la ville
C'est la Nouvelle Quelque Chose travaillée au socle et à l'archet de
    l'arche
L'air est taillé comme un diamant
Pour les peignes de l'immense Vierge en proie à des vertiges
    d'essence alcoolique ou florale
15   La douce cataracte gronde de parfums sur les travaux[3]

for Francis Picabia[1]

It too is the penitentiary with its breaches as blond as a book on a
    girl's knees
It is closed for now and bursts with future distress[2] on the eddies of
    a sheer sea
A long silence followed these murders
The silver is drying on the rocks
5   Then in the guise of beauty or reason contrary also to all guises
And both hands in a single palm
Evening is seen
Falling pearl necklace from the peaks
Over the spirit of those spotted tribes such a plaintive love reigns
10   That the soothsayers begin snickering loudly on the iron bridges
The little statues hold hands across the city
It's the New Something whose base and arch's bow are wrought
The air is cut like a diamond
For the combs of the immense Virgin in the throes of dizzy spells of
    alcoholic or floral essence
15   The gentle cataract rumbles with fragrances on the worksite[3]

(JPC)

Rendez-vous

à T. Fraenkel

Après les tempêtes cerclées de verre, l'éclair à l'armure brouillée et cette enjambée silencieuse sous laquelle la montagne ouvre des yeux plus fascinants que le Siam, petite fille, adoratrice du pays calqué sur tes parfums, tu vas surprendre l'éveil des chercheurs dans un air révolutionné par le platine. De loin la statue rose qui porte à bout de bras une sorte de bouteille fumant dans un panier regarde par-dessus son épaule errer les anciens vanniers et acrobates. Un joli bagne d'artistes où des zèbres bleus, fouettés par les soupirs qui s'enroulent le soir autour des arbres, exécutent sans fin leur numéro! D'étonnants faisceaux, formés au bord des routes avec les bobines d'azur et le télégraphe, répondent de ta sécurité. Là, dans la lumière profane, les seins éclatant sous un globe de rosée et t'abandonnant à la glissière infinie, à travers les bambous froids tu verras passer le Prince Vandale. L'occasion brûlera aux quatre vents de soufre, de cadmium, de sel et de Bengale. Le bombyx à tête humaine étouffera peu à peu les arlequins maudits et les grandes catastrophes ressusciteront pêle-mêle, pour se résorber dans la bague au chaton vide que je t'ai donnée et qui te tuera.

Rendez-vous

for T. Fraenkel

After the glass-ringed tempests, the flash of blurred armor and that silent stride beneath which the mountain opens eyes more fascinating than Siam, little girl, worshipper of the country transposed from your fragrances, you go forth and surprise the prospectors' awakening in a platinum-revolutionized air. From afar, the pink statue holding at arm's length a sort of bottle smoking in a basket looks back over its shoulder and sees the old-time basket weavers and acrobats wandering. A pretty artists' penitentiary where blue zebras, flogged by sighs that coil around trees, endlessly perform their act! Astonishing sheaves formed at the road's edge by azure spools and the telegraph answer for your security. There, in the profane light, breasts bursting under an orb of dew and surrendering you to an infinite slide, through cold bamboo stalks you shall see the Vandal Prince pass by. The occasion will burn in the four winds of sulphur, cadmium, salt and Bengal. The bombyx with its human head will gradually stifle the accursed harlequins, and large-scale catastrophes will resurrect pell-mell, then be resorbed into the ring with the empty setting that I gave you and that will kill you.

(JPC)

Privé[I]

Coiffé d'une cape beige, il caracole sur l'affiche de satin où deux plumes de paradis lui tiennent lieu d'éperons. Elle, de ses jointures spéciales en haut des airs part la chanson des espèces rayonnantes. Ce qui reste du moteur sanglant est envahi par l'aubépine: à cette heure les premiers scaphandriers tombent du ciel. La température s'est brusquement adoucie et chaque matin la légèreté secoue sur nos toits ses cheveux d'ange. Contre les maléfices à quoi bon ce petit chien bleuâtre au corps pris dans un solénoïde de verre noir? Et pour une fois ne se peut-il que l'expression *pour la vie* déclenche une des aurores boréales dont sera fait le tapis de table du Jugement Dernier?

Private[1]

With a beige cape on his head, he prances about on the satin poster where two paradise feathers serve his purpose instead of spurs. As for her, from her special joints in the high-pitched air the song of radiating species issues forth. What remains of the blood-stained engine is over-grown with hawthorn: at this time the first deep sea divers fall from the sky. The temperature has suddenly become milder and each morning lightness shakes her angel hair over our roofs. To counter evil spells, of what avail this little bluish dog with its body caught in a solenoid of black glass? And for once can it not be that the phrase *for a lifetime* triggers one of the northern lights of which the Last Judgment's table cover will be made?

(JPC)

Le Buvard de cendre

à Robert Desnos

Les oiseaux s'ennuieront

Si j'avais oublié quelque chose

Sonnez la cloche de ces sorties d'école dans la mer
Ce que nous appellerons la bourrache pensive

5   On commence par donner la solution du concours
A savoir combien de larmes peuvent tenir dans une main de femme
1° aussi petite que possible
2° dans une main moyenne

Tandis que je froisse ce journal étoilé
10   Et que les chairs éternelles entrées une fois pour toutes en possession
      du sommet des montagnes
J'habite sauvagement une petite maison du Vaucluse

Cœur lettre de cachet[1]

Cinder Blotter

for Robert Desnos

Birds will be bored

If I'd forgotten something

Ring the bells of those school dismissals in the sea
What we shall call pensive borage

5   We start by giving the solution to the contest
To wit how many tears can be held in a woman's hand
1. as little as possible
2. in a medium-sized hand

While I crumple this star-lit paper
10   And while the everlasting flesh has once and for all taken possession
      of the mountain summits
I live like a recluse in a little house in the Vaucluse

Heart king's order[1]

(MAC)

Tout paradis n'est pas perdu

à Man Ray

Les coqs de roche passent dans le cristal
Ils défendent la rosée à coups de crête
Alors la devise charmante de l'éclair
Descend sur la bannière des ruines
5   Le sable n'est plus qu'une horloge phosphorescente
Qui dit minuit
Par les bras d'une femme oubliée
Point de refuge[I] tournant dans la campagne
Dressée aux approches et aux reculs célestes
10 C'est ici
Les tempes bleues et dures de la villa baignent dans la nuit qui
        décalque mes images
Chevelures chevelures
Le mal prend des forces tout près
Seulement voudra-t-il de nous

No Paradise is Lost

for Man Ray

Rock roosters pass into crystal
They defend the dew with thrusts of their combs
So the charming motto of the lightning
Descends upon the ruins' banner
5   Sand is but a phosphorescent clock
That says midnight
By the arms of a forgotten woman
No refuge¹ turning in the countryside
Erected in far and near celestial reaches
10   Here it is
The villa's hard blue temples are steeped in the night that traces out
    my images
Tresses tresses
Evil draws its strength close by
But will it need us

(JPC)

Silhouette de paille

à Max Ernst

Donnez-moi des bijoux de noyées
Deux crèches
Une prêle et une marotte de modiste
Ensuite pardonnez-moi
5   Je n'ai pas le temps de respirer
Je suis un sort
La construction solaire m'a retenu jusqu'ici
Maintenant je n'ai plus qu'à laisser mourir
Demandez le barème
10 Au trot le poing fermé au-dessus de ma tête qui sonne
Un verre dans lequel s'ouvre un œil jaune
Le sentiment s'ouvre aussi
Mais les princesses s'accrochent à l'air pur
J'ai besoin d'orgueil
15 Et de quelques gouttes plates
Pour réchauffer la marmite de fleurs moisies
Au pied de l'escalier
Pensée divine au carreau étoilé de ciel bleu
L'expression des baigneuses c'est la mort du loup
20 Prenez-moi pour amie
L'amie des feux et des furets
Vous regarde à deux fois
Lissez vos peines
Ma rame de palissandre fait chanter vos cheveux
25 Un son palpable dessert[1] la plage
Noire de la colère des seiches
Et rouge du côté du panonceau

Straw Silhouette

for Max Ernst

Give me drowned women's jewels
Two cribs
A horsetail plant and a milliner's dummy head
Then pardon me
5 I don't have the time to breathe
I am a spell
Solar construction has thus far detained me
Now I can only let die
Ask for the chart
10 Quickly with clenched fist above my ringing head
A glass in which a yellow eye opens
Feeling also opens up
But princesses hang on to pure air
I need pride
15 And a few flat drops
To warm up the kettle of musty flowers
At the foot of the staircase
Divine thought whose tile is star-studded with blue sky
The expression of bathers is a wolf's death
20 Take me for your girl friend
The girl friend of fires and ferrets
Looks at you twice over
Smooth out your woes
My rosewood paddle makes your hair sing
25 A palpable sound clears^{I} the beach
Black with cuttle-fish anger
And red on the side of the sign

(JPC)

Mille et mille fois

à Francis Picabia!

Sous le couvert des pas qui regagnent le soir une tour habitée par des
    signes mystérieux au nombre de onze
La neige que je prends dans la main et qui fond
Cette neige que j'adore fait des rêves et je suis un de ces rêves
Moi qui n'accorde au jour et à la nuit que la stricte jeunesse
    nécessaire
5   Ce sont deux jardins dans lesquels se promènent mes mains qui n'ont
    rien à faire
Et pendant que les onze signes se reposent
Je prends part à l'amour qui est une mécanique de cuivre et d'argent
    dans la haie
Je suis un des rouages les plus délicats de l'amour terrestre
Et l'amour terrestre cache les autres amours
10   A la façon des signes qui me cachent l'esprit
Un coup de couteau perdu siffle à l'oreille du promeneur
J'ai défait le ciel comme un lit merveilleux
Mon bras pend du ciel avec un chapelet d'étoiles
Qui descend de jour en jour
15   Et dont le premier grain va disparaître dans la mer
A la place de mes couleurs vivantes
Il n'y aura bientôt plus que de la neige sur la mer
Les signes apparaissent à la porte
Ils sont de onze couleurs différentes et leurs dimensions respectives
    vous feraient mourir de pitié
20   L'un d'eux est obligé de se baisser et de se croiser les bras pour entrer
    dans la tour
J'entends l'autre qui brûle dans une région prospère
Et celui-ci à cheval sur l'industrie la rare industrie montagneuse
Pareille à l'onagre qui se nourrit de truites
Les cheveux les longs cheveux pommelés

A Thousand Times and More

for Francis Picabia

Under cover of steps returning in the evening to a tower inhabited
  by mysterious signs eleven in number
The snow that I grasp in my hand and that melts
This snow that I adore has dreams and I am one of those dreams
I who do not concede to day or night any more youthfulness than
  is necessary
5   They are two gardens in which my hands with nothing to do stroll
And while the eleven signs take a rest
I share in love which is a mechanism of copper and silver in the
  hedge
I am one of the most delicate cogs of earthly love
And earthly love hides other loves
10   In the manner of signs that hide the spirit from me
The stray thrust of a knife whistles in the stroller's ear
I've unmade the sky like a marvelous bed
My arm hangs from the sky with a rosary of stars
That descends from day to day
15   And whose first bead is going to disappear into the sea
Instead of my lively colors
There shall soon be only snow upon the sea
Signs appear at the door
They are in eleven different colors and their respective dimensions
  would make you die of pity
20   One of them is obliged to bend down and to fold its arms in order
  to enter the tower
I hear the other one burning in a prosperous region
And this one on horseback astride industry rare mountain
  industry
Similar to the onager feeding on trout
Hair long dappled gray hair

25   Caractérisent le signe qui porte le bouclier doublement ogival
      Il faut se méfier de l'idée que roulent les torrents
      Ma construction ma belle construction page à page
      Maison insensément vitrée à ciel ouvert à sol ouvert
      C'est une faille dans le roc suspendu par des anneaux à la tringle
          du monde
30   C'est un rideau métallique qui se baisse sur des inscriptions divines
      Que vous ne savez pas lire
      Les signes n'ont jamais affecté que moi
      Je prends naissance dans le désordre infini des prières
      Je vis et je meurs d'un bout à l'autre de cette ligne
35   Cette ligne étrangement mesurée qui relie mon cœur à l'appui de
          votre fenêtre
      Je corresponds par elle avec tous les prisonniers du monde

25   Characterizes the sign bearing the double-ogive shield
      Beware of an idea driven by torrents
      My construction my beautiful construction page by page
      Absurdly glass-wrought house facing open sky open earth
      It's a fault in the rock hanging by rings from the rod of the world
30   It's a metallic curtain that drops on divine inscriptions
      That you don't know how to read
      Signs have never affected anyone but me
      I am born in the infinite disorder of prayers
      I live and die from one end of this line to the other
35   This strangely measured line that links my heart to your window
         ledge
      I correspond thereby with all the world's prisoners

(JPC)

Ligne brisée

à Raymond Roussel

Nous le pain sec et l'eau dans les prisons du ciel
Nous les pavés de l'amour tous les signaux interrompus
Qui personnifions les grâces de ce poème
Rien ne nous exprime au-delà de la mort
5   A cette heure où la nuit pour sortir met ses bottines vernies
Nous prenons le temps comme il vient
Comme un mur mitoyen à celui de nos prisons
Les araignées font entrer le bateau dans la rade
Il n'y a qu'à toucher il n'y a rien à voir
10   Plus tard vous apprendrez qui nous sommes
Nos travaux sont encore bien défendus
Mais c'est l'aube de la dernière côte le temps se gâte
Bientôt nous porterons ailleurs notre luxe embarrassant
Nous porterons ailleurs le luxe de la peste
15   Nous un peu de gelée blanche sur les fagots humains
Et c'est tout
L'eau-de-vie panse les blessures dans un caveau par le soupirail
      duquel on aperçoit une route bordée de grandes patiences[I] vides
Ne demandez pas où vous êtes
Nous le pain sec et l'eau dans les prisons du ciel
20   Le jeu de cartes à la belle étoile
Nous soulevons à peine un coin du voile
Le raccommodeur de faïence travaille sur une échelle
Il paraît jeune en dépit de la concession
Nous portons son deuil en jaune
25   Le pacte n'est pas encore signé
Les sœurs de charité provoquent
A l'horizon des fuites
Peut-être pallions-nous à la fois le mal et le bien
C'est ainsi que la volonté des rêves se fait

Broken Line

for Raymond Roussel

We plain bread and water in the prisons of the sky
We the paving stones of love all the interrupted signals
Who personify the charms of this poem
Nothing expresses us beyond death
5   At this hour when night puts on its polished ankle-boots to go out
We take our time as it comes
Like a party wall adjoining that of our prisons
Spiders bring the ship into the harbor
One has only to touch there is nothing to see
10   Later you shall learn who we are
Our labors are still well protected
But it's dawn on the last shore the weather is worsening
Soon we'll carry our cumbersome luxury elsewhere
We'll carry the luxury of the plague elsewhere
15   We a little hoarfrost on human firewood
And that's all
Brandy dresses wounds in a cellar through the vent from which one
    glimpses a road lined with great empty patience-docks[I]
Don't ask where you are
We plain bread and water in the prisons of the sky
20   Card game under the stars
We scarcely lift the veil by its edge
The mender of crockery is working on a ladder
He looks young despite the concession
We wear yellow mourning for him
25   The pact is not yet signed
The sisters of charity provoke
Escapes on the horizon
Perhaps we palliate at the same time evil and good
Thus it is that the will of dreams is done

30   Gens qui pourriez
      Nos rigueurs se perdent dans le regret des émiettements
      Nous sommes les vedettes de la séduction plus terrible
      Le croc du chiffonnier Matin sur les hardes fleuries
      Nous jette â la fureur des trésors aux dents longues
35   N'ajoutez rien à la honte de votre propre pardon
      C'est assez que d'armer pour une fin sans fond
      Vos yeux de ces larmes ridicules qui nous soulagent
      Le ventre des mots est doré ce soir et rien n'est plus en vain

30 People you who could
    Our rigors become lost in the regret of all that crumbles
    We are the popular idols of the more terrible seduction
    Ragman Morning's hook on flowery tatters
    Casts us to the fury of long-toothed treasures
35 Don't add anything to the shame of your own pardon
    'Tis enough to arm toward a bottomless end
    Your eyes with these ridiculous tears that relieve us
    The belly of words is golden this evening and nothing is in vain
       any more

(JPC)

Tournesol[I]

à Pierre Reverdy

La voyageuse qui traversa les Halles[2] à la tombée de l'été
Marchait sur la pointe des pieds
Le désespoir roulait au ciel ses grands arums si beaux
Et dans le sac à main il y avait mon rêve ce flacon de sels
5   Que seule a respirés la marraine de Dieu
Les torpeurs se déployaient comme la buée
Au Chien qui fume[3]
Où venaient d'entrer le pour et le contre
La jeune femme ne pouvait être vue d'eux que mal et de biais
10   Avais-je affaire à l'ambassadrice du salpêtre
Ou de la courbe blanche sur fond noir que nous appelons pensée
Le bal des innocents[4] battait son plein
Les lampions prenaient feu lentement dans les marronniers
La dame sans ombre s'agenouilla sur le Pont au Change
15   Rue Gît-le-Cœur les timbres n'étaient plus les mêmes
Les promesses des nuits étaient enfin tenues
Les pigeons voyageurs les baisers de secours
Se joignaient aux seins de la belle inconnue
Dardés sous le crêpe des significations parfaites
20   Une ferme prospérait en plein Paris
Et ses fenêtres donnaient sur la voie lactée
Mais personne ne l'habitait encore à cause des survenants
Des survenants qu'on sait plus dévoués que les revenants
Les uns comme cette femme ont l'air de nager
25   Et dans l'amour il entre un peu de leur substance
Elle les intériorise
Je ne suis le jouet d'aucune puissance sensorielle
Et pourtant le grillon qui chantait dans les cheveux de cendre
Un soir près de la statue d'Etienne Marcel
30   M'a jeté un coup d'œil d'intelligence
André Breton a-t-il dit passe

◀   74

Sunflower[1]

for Pierre Reverdy

The woman on her journey who passed through the Halles[2] at
    summer's fall
Was walking on tiptoe
In the sky despair was sweeping its great lovely calla lilies
And in the handbag there was my dream that flask of salts
5   Breathed solely by God's godmother
Torpor fanned out like mist
At the Chien qui fume café[3]
Where pro and con had just entered
The young woman could hardly be seen and only askance
10   Was I dealing with the ambassadress of saltpeter
Or of the white curve on a black background that we call thought
The innocents'[4] ball was in full swing
The Chinese lanterns slowly caught fire among the chestnut trees
The shadowless lady knelt down on the Pont au Change
15   In the Rue Gît-le-Cœur the tones no longer had the same ring
Nighttime pledges were fulfilled at last
Homing pigeons emergency kisses
Joined the beautiful stranger's breasts
Pointed under the crepe of perfect meanings
20   A farm was prospering in the very heart of Paris
And its windows looked out on the Milky Way
But no one lived there yet because of unexpected callers
Drop-in guests known to be more devoted than ghosts
A few like that woman seem to be swimming
25   And in love there enters some of their substance
She interiorizes them
I am the pawn of no sensory power
And yet the cricket singing in the ashen hair
One evening near the statue of Etienne Marcel
30   Gave me a knowing look
André Breton it said pass on

(JPC)

From *Poisson soluble*
[Soluble Fish]
1924

Moins de temps qu'il n'en faut pour le dire, moins de larmes qu'il n'en faut pour mourir; j'ai tout compté, voilà. J'ai fait le recensement des pierres; elles sont au nombre de mes doigts et de quelques autres; j'ai distribué des prospectus aux plantes, mais toutes n'ont pas voulu les accepter. Avec la musique j'ai lié partie pour une seconde seulement et maintenant je ne sais plus que penser du suicide, car si je veux me séparer de moi-même, la sortie est de ce côté et, j'ajoute malicieusement: l'entrée, la rentrée de cet autre côté. Tu vois ce qu'il te reste à faire. Les heures, le chagrin, je n'en tiens pas un compte raisonnable; je suis seul, je regarde par la fenêtre; il ne passe personne, ou plutôt personne ne *passe* (je souligne passe). Ce Monsieur, vous ne le connaissez pas? c'est M. Lemême. Je vous présente Madame Madame. Et leurs enfants. Puis je reviens sur mes pas, mes pas reviennent aussi, mais je ne sais pas exactement sur quoi ils reviennent. Je consulte un horaire; les noms de villes ont été remplacés par des noms de personnes qui m'ont touché d'assez près. Irai-je à A, retournerai-je à B, changerai-je à X? Oui, naturellement je changerai à X. Pourvu que je ne manque pas la correspondance avec l'ennui! Nous y sommes: l'ennui, les belles parallèles, ah! que les parallèles sont belles sous la perpendiculaire de Dieu.

Less time than it takes to say it, less tears than it takes to die; I've taken account of everything, there you have it. I've made a census of the stones; they are as numerous as my fingers and some others; I've distributed some pamphlets to the plants, but not all were willing to accept them. I've kept company with music for a second only and now I no longer know what to think of suicide, for if I want to part from myself, the exit is on this side and, I add mischievously, the entrance, the re-entrance on the other. You see what you still have to do. Hours, grief, I don't keep a reasonable account of them; I'm alone, I look out of the window; there is no passerby, or rather no one *passes* (underline passes). You don't know this man? It's Mr. Same. May I introduce Madam Madam? And their children. Then I turn back on my steps, my steps turn back too, but I don't know exactly what they turn back on. I consult a schedule; the names of towns have been replaced by the names of people who have been quite close to me. Shall I go to A, return to B, change at X? Yes, of course I'll change at X. Provided I don't miss the connection with boredom! There we are: boredom, beautiful parallels, ah! how beautiful the parallels are under God's perpendicular.

(JPC)

à Antonin Artaud

Sale nuit, nuit de fleurs, nuit de râles,[1] nuit capiteuse, nuit sourde dont la main est un cerf-volant abject retenu par des fils de tous côtés, des fils noirs, des fils honteux![2] Campagne d'os blancs et rouges, qu'as-tu fait de tes arbres immondes, de ta candeur arborescente, de ta fidélité qui était une bourse aux perles serrées, avec des fleurs, des inscriptions comme ci comme ça, des significations à tout prendre?[3] Et toi, bandit, bandit, ah! tu me tues,[4] bandit de l'eau qui effeuilles tes couteaux dans mes yeux, tu n'as donc pitié de rien, eau rayonnante, eau lustrale que je chéris! Mes imprécations vous poursuivront longtemps comme une enfant jolie à faire peur qui agite dans votre direction son balai de genêt.[5] Au bout de chaque branche, il y a une étoile et ce n'est pas assez, non, chicorée de la Vierge.[6] Je ne veux plus vous voir, je veux cribler de petits plombs vos oiseaux qui ne sont même plus des feuilles, je veux vous chasser de ma porte, cœurs à pépins, cervelles d'amour. Assez de crocodiles là-bas, assez de dents de crocodile sur les cuirasses de guerriers samouraïs, assez de jets d'encre enfin, et des renégats partout, des renégats à manchettes[7] pourpres, des renégats à œil de cassis, à cheveux de poule![8] C'est fini, je ne cacherai plus ma honte, je ne serai plus calmé par rien, par moins que rien. Et si les volants sont grands comme des maisons, comment voulez-vous que nous jouiions, que nous entretenions notre vermine, que nous placions nos mains[9] sur les lèvres des coquilles qui parlent sans cesse (ces coquilles, qui les fera taire, enfin?) Plus de souffles, plus de sang, plus d'âme, mais des mains pour pétrir l'air, pour dorer une seule fois le pain de l'air, pour faire claquer la grande gomme des drapeaux qui dorment, des mains solaires, enfin, des main gelées!

for Antonin Artaud

Night of filth, night of flowers, night of groans,[1] giddy night, muffled night whose hand is an abject kite held back by strings on all sides, black strings, shameful strings![2] Countryside of white and red bones, what have you done with your horrendous trees, your arborescent candor, your fidelity that was once a purse of serried pearls, flowers and inscriptions scattered here and there, meanings, taking one thing with another?[3] And you, bandit, bandit, oh! you slay me,[4] water bandit defoliating your knives in my eyes, don't you take pity on anything, radiant water, lustral water that I cherish! My imprecations will hound you for ages like a frighteningly pretty child brandishing after you its flowering broom.[5] At the tip of each branch, there is a star and that is not all, no, succory of the Virgin.[6] I want to see you never again, to riddle with buckshot your birds that aren't even leaves any longer, to chase you from my door, hearts with pips, brains of love. Enough crocodiles over there, enough crocodile teeth on the breastplates of samurai warriors, enough ink spurts, and renegades everywhere, renegades with purple cuffs,[7] with black-currant eyes, with chicken hair![8] That's done with, I'll hide my shame no more, nothing will calm me, less than nothing. And if the shutters are as high as houses, how do you expect us to play, or maintain our vermin, or lay our hands[9] on the lips of ever-babbling shells (these shells, who will silence them at last?) No more breath, no more blood, no more soul, but hands to knead the air, to make the bread of air golden only once, to flap the great gum of sleeping flags, solar hands, in short, frozen hands!

(MAC)

On s'est avisé un jour de recueillir dans une coupe de terre blanche le duvet des fruits; cette buée on en a enduit plusieurs miroirs et l'on est revenu bien longtemps après. Les miroirs avaient disparu. Les miroirs s'étaient levés l'un après l'autre et étaient sortis en tremblant. Beaucoup plus tard encore, quelqu'un confessa que, rentrant de son travail, il avait rencontré l'un de ces miroirs qui s'était approché insensiblement et qu'il avait emmené chez lui. C'était un jeune apprenti fort beau sous sa cotte rose qui le faisait ressembler à une cuve pleine d'eau dans laquelle on a lavé une blessure. La tête de cette eau avait souri comme mille oiseaux dans un arbre aux racines immergées. Il avait monté sans peine le miroir chez lui et il se souvenait seulement que deux portes qui présentaient chacune une plaque de verre étroit encadrant la poignée. Il tenait les deux bras écartés pour soutenir son fardeau qu'il déposa avec précautions dans un angle de l'unique pièce qu'il occupait au septième étage puis il se coucha. Il ne ferma pas les yeux de la nuit; le miroir se reflétait lui-même à une profondeur inconnue, à une distance incroyable. Les villes n'avaient que le temps d'apparaître entre ces deux épaisseurs: villes de fièvre sillonnées en tous sens par des femmes seules, villes d'abandon, de génie aussi, dont les édifices étaient surmontés de statues animées, dont les monte-charges étaient construits à la ressemblance humaine, villes d'orages pauvres et celle-ci plus belle et plus fugitive que les autres dont tous les palais, toutes les usines étaient en forme de fleurs: la violette était le lieu d'attache des bateaux. Sur le revers des villes, il n'y avait en guise de campagnes que des ciels, ciels mecaniques, ciels chimiques, ciels mathématiques, où évoluaient les figures du zodiaque, chacune dans leur élément, mais les Gémeaux revenaient plus souvent que les autres. Le jeune homme se leva précipitamment vers une heure, persuadé que le miroir penchait en avant et allait tomber. Il le remit d'aplomb avec beaucoup de difficulté et, soudain inquiet, il jugea périlleux de regagner son lit et demeura assis sur une chaise boiteuse, à un pas seulement du miroir et bien en face de lui. Il crut alors surprendre dans la pièce une respiration étrangère, mais non, rien. Il voyait maintenant un jeune homme sous une grande porte, ce jeune homme était à peu près

One day someone fancied gathering in a bowl of white earth the fuzz of fruit, misting several mirrors with it and came back much later. The mirrors had disappeared. The mirrors had gotten up one after the other and had gone out trembling. Much later yet, someone confessed that, coming home from work, he had encountered one of the mirrors that had gotten imperceptibly closer and that he had taken to his home. It was a young apprentice, very handsome underneath his pink overalls that made him look like a vat full of water in which a wound has been cleansed. The water's head had smiled like a thousand birds in a tree with immersed roots. He had effortlessly carried the mirror to his house and remembered that only two doors had slammed as he went through, two doors each of which bore a plate of narrow glass framing the handle. He held his two arms apart to hold up his burden which he put down carefully in a corner of the single room he occupied on the seventh floor, then went to bed. He didn't shut his eyes the whole night; the mirror reflected itself to an unknown depth, at an incredible distance. Cities had just enough time to appear between these two thicknesses, cities of fever criss-crossed in every direction by single women, cities of abandon, of genius too, whose edifices were surmounted with animated statues, whose dumbwaiters were built in a human semblance, cities of poor storms and this one more beautiful and more fleeting than the others all of whose palaces, all of whose factories were shaped like flowers: the violet was the mooring place of ships. On the reverse side of cities, there were by way of countryside only skies, mechanical skies, chemical skies, mathematical skies, where the figures of the zodiac moved about, each one in its element, but Gemini recurred more often than the others. The young man got up hurriedly at approximately one o'clock, convinced that the mirror was leaning forward and was about to fall. He set it upright with great difficulty and, suddenly anxious, thought it risky to go back to bed and remained seated on a wobbly chair, one step away from the mirror and facing it squarely. He thought he sensed in the room someone else breathing, but no, nothing. He now saw a young man beneath a large door, the young man was almost naked; there was

nu; il n'y avait derrière lui qu'un paysage noir qui pouvait être de papier brûlé. Les formes seules des objets subsistaient et il était possible de reconnaître les substances dans lesquelles ces objets s'étaient moulés. Rien de plus tragique, en vérité. Quelques-unes de ces choses lui avaient appartenu: bijoux, présents d'amour, reliques de l'enfance, et jusqu'à ce petit flacon de parfum dont le bouchon était introuvable. D'autres lui étaient inconnus et il n'en pouvait démêler l'usage à venir, sans doute. L'apprenti regardait toujours plus loin dans la cendre. Il éprouvait une satisfaction coupable à voir s'approcher de ses mains ce jeune homme souriant dont le visage était pareil à un globe à l'intérieur duquel voletaient deux oiseaux-mouches. Il lui avait pris la taille qui était celle du miroir, n'est-ce pas, et, les oiseaux enfuis, la musique montait dans leur sillage. Que se passa-t-il jamais dans cette chambre? Toujours est-il que depuis ce jour le miroir n'a point été retrouvé et que ce n'est jamais sans émotion que j'approche la bouche d'un de ses éclats possibles, quitte à ne plus voir enfin apparaître ces bagues de duvet, les cygnes sur le point de chanter.

behind him but a black landscape that might have been charred paper. Only the shape of the objects subsisted and it was possible to recognize the substances in which these objects had molded themselves. In truth, nothing more tragic. Some of these things had belonged to him; jewels, love gifts, childhood relics, even the little perfume flask whose stopper was nowhere to be found. Others were unknown to him and he couldn't fathom their future use, most likely. The apprentice kept looking ever further in the ashes. He felt a guilty satisfaction at seeing the smiling young man getting close to his hands, his face like a globe inside which two hummingbirds flitted about. He had clasped his waist that was that of the mirror, you understand, and, once the birds had flown, the music grew louder in their wake. What ever happened in that room? All that is known is that since that day the mirror has not been found and that it is never without emotion that I bring my mouth close to one of its possible shards, at the risk of not finally seeing appear those rings of down, swans on the verge of singing.

(JPC)

Il y avait une fois un dindon sur une digue. Ce dindon n'avait plus que quelques jours à s'allumer au grand soleil et il se regardait avec mystère dans une glace de Venise disposée à cet effet sur la digue. C'est ici qu'intervient la main de l'homme, cette fleur des champs dont vous n'êtes pas sans avoir entendu parler. Le dindon, qui répondait au nom de Troisétoiles, en manière de plaisanterie, ne savait plus où donner de la tête. Chacun sait que la tête des dindons est un prisme à sept ou huit faces tout comme le chapeau haut de forme est un prisme à sept ou huit reflets.

Le chapeau haut de forme se balançait sur la digue à la façon d'une moule énorme qui chante sur un rocher. La digue n'avait aucune raison d'être depuis que la mer s'était retirée, avec force, ce matin-là. Le port était, d'ailleurs, éclairé tout entier par une lampe à arc de la grandeur d'un enfant qui va à l'école.

Le dindon se sentait perdu s'il n'arrivait pas à émouvoir ce passant. L'enfant vit le chapeau haut de forme et, comme il avait faim, il entreprit de le vider de son contenu, en l'espèce une belle méduse à bec papillon. Les papillons peuvent-ils être assimilés à des lumières? Evidemment; c'est pourquoi l'enterrement s'arrêta sur la digue. Le prêtre chantait dans la moule, la moule chantait dans la mer et la mer chantait dans la mer.

Aussi le dindon est-il resté sur la digue, et depuis ce jour fait-il peur à l'enfant qui va à l'ecole.

There was once a turkey on a sea wall. The turkey had but a few days to light up in the full sun and it gazed upon itself with mystery in a Venetian mirror set up for that purpose on a sea wall. At this point the hand of man comes in, that meadow flower that you have heard about. The turkey, who answered to the name of Threestars, as a joke, didn't know which way to turn. Everyone knows that a turkey's head is a prism with seven or eight faces just as a tophat is a prism with seven with seven or eight reflections.

The tophat swayed on the sea wall in the manner of a huge mussel singing on a rock. The sea wall had no reason to be since the sea had forcibly receded that very morning. As is happens, the port was illuminated in its entirety by an arc lamp the size of a child going to school.

The turkey felt at a loss if it didn't manage to move this passerby. The child saw the tophat and, being hungry, undertook to empty it of its contents, which happened to be an attractive jellyfish with a butterfly burner. Can butterflies be likened to lights? Evidently; which is why the burial stopped on the sea wall. The priest sang in the mussel, the mussel sang in the sea, and the sea sang in the sea.

The turkey thus remained on the sea wall, and since that day has frightened the child going to school.

(JPC)

L'Union libre [Free Union]
1931

L'Union libre[1]

Ma femme à la chevelure de feu de bois
Aux pensées d'éclairs de chaleur
A la taille de sablier
Ma femme à la taille de loutre entre les dents du tigre
5   Ma femme à la bouche de cocarde et de bouquet d'étoiles de dernière
     grandeur
Aux dents d'empreintes de souris blanche sur la terre blanche
A la langue d'ambre et de verre frottés
Ma femme à la langue d'hostie poignardée
A la langue de poupée qui ouvre et ferme les yeux
10 A la langue de pierre incroyable
Ma femme aux cils de bâtons d'écriture d'enfant
Aux sourcils de bord de nid d'hirondelle
Ma femme aux tempes d'ardoise de toit de serre
Et de buée aux vitres
15 Ma femme aux épaules de champagne
Et de fontaine à têtes de dauphins sous la glace
Ma femme aux poignets d'allumettes
Ma femme aux doigts de hasard et d'as de cœur
Aux doigts de foin coupé
20 Ma femme aux aisselles de martre et de fênes[2]
De nuit de la Saint-Jean
De troène et de nid de scalares[3]
Aux bras d'écume de mer et d'écluse
Et de mélange du blé et du moulin
25 Ma femme aux jambes de fusée
Aux mouvements d'horlogerie[4] et de désespoir
Ma femme aux mollets de moelle de sureau
Ma femme aux pieds d'initiales[5]
Aux pieds de trousseaux de clés aux pieds de calfats[6] qui boivent

Free Union[1]

My love whose hair is woodfire
Her thoughts heat lightning
Her hourglass waist
An otter in the tiger's jaws my love
5 Her mouth a rosette bouquet of stars of the highest magnitude
The footprints of white mice on the white earth her teeth
Her tongue rubbed amber and glass
My love her tongue a sacred host stabbed through
Her tongue a doll whose eyes close and open
10 Her tongue an incredible stone
A child's hand traced each eyelash
Her eyebrows the edge of a swallow's nest
My love her temples slates on a greenhouse roof
And their misted panes
15 My love whose shoulders are champagne
And dolphin heads of a fountain under ice
My love her matchthin wrists
Whose fingers are chance and the ace of hearts
Whose fingers are mowed hay
20 My love with marten and beechnut beneath her arms[2]
Midsummer night
Of privet and the nests of angel fish[3]
Whose arms are seafoam and river locks
And of the mingling of wheat and mill
25 Whose legs are Roman candles
Moving like clockwork[4] and despair
Marrow of eldertree
My love whose feet are initials[5]
Key rings and Java sparrows[6] drinking

30 Ma femme au cou d'orge imperlé[7]
    Ma femme à la gorge de Val d'or
    De rendez-vous dans le lit même du torrent
    Aux seins de nuit
    Ma femme aux seins de taupinière marine
35 Ma femme aux seins de creuset du rubis
    Aux seins de spectre de la rose sous la rosée
    Ma femme au ventre de dépliement d'éventail des jours
    Au ventre de griffe géante
    Ma femme au dos d'oiseau qui fuit vertical
40 Au dos de vif-argent
    Au dos de lumière
    A la nuque de pierre roulée et de craie mouillée
    Et de chute d'un verre dans lequel on vient de boire
    Ma femme aux hanches de nacelle
45 Aux hanches de lustre et de pennes de flèche
    Et de tiges de plumes de paon blanc
    De balance insensible
    Ma femme aux fesses de grès et d'amiante
    Ma femme aux fesses de dos de cygne
50 Ma femme aux fesses de printemps
    Au sexe de glaïeul
    Ma femme au sexe de placer et d'ornithorynque
    Ma femme au sexe d'algue et de bonbons anciens
    Ma femme au sexe de miroir
55 Ma femme aux yeux pleins de larmes
    Aux yeux de panoplie violette et d'aiguille aimantée
    Ma femme aux yeux de savane
    Ma femme aux yeux d'eau pour boire en prison
    Ma femme aux yeux de bois toujours sous la hache
60 Aux yeux de niveau d'eau de niveau d'air de terre et de feu

30   My love her neck pearled with barley [7]
     My love a golden-throated town
     Rendez-vous in the torrent's very bed
     Her breasts of night
     Her breasts molehills under the sea
35   Crucibles of rubies
     Spectre of the dewsparkled rose
     Whose belly unfurls the fan of every day
     Its giant claws
     Whose back is a bird's vertical flight
40   Whose back is quicksilver
     Whose back is light
     The nape of her neck is crushed stone and damp chalk
     And the fall of a glass where we just drank
     My love whose hips are skiffs on high
45   Whose hips are chandeliers and arrow feathers
     And the stems of white peacock plumes
     Imperceptible in their sway
     My love whose buttocks are of sandstone
     Of swan's back and amianthus
50   And of springtime
     My love whose sex is swordlily
     Is placer and platypus
     Algae and sweets of yore
     Is mirror
55   Eyes full of tears
     Of violet-panoply and magnetic needle
     My love of savannah eyes
     Of eyes of water to drink in prison
     Eyes of wood always to be chopped
60   Eyes of water level earth and air and fire

(MAC and PT)

From *Le Revolver à cheveux blancs*
[The White-Haired Revolver]
1932

Non-lieu

Art des jours art des nuits
La balance des blessures qui s'appelle Pardonne
Balance rouge et sensible au poids d'un vol d'oiseau
Quand les écuyères au col de neige les mains vides
5   Poussent leurs chars de vapeur sur les prés
Cette balance sans cesse affolée je la vois
Je vois l'ibis aux belles manières
Qui revient de l'étang lacé dans mon cœur
Les roues du rêve charment les splendides ornières
10   Qui se lèvent très haut sur les coquilles de leurs robes
Et l'étonnement bondit de-ci de-là sur la mer
Partez ma chère aurore n'oubliez rien de ma vie
Prenez ces roses qui grimpent au puits des miroirs
Prenez les battements de tous les cils
15   Prenez jusqu'aux fils qui soutiennent les pas des danseurs de corde et
        des gouttes d'eau
Art des jours art des nuits
Je suis à la fenêtre très loin dans une cité pleine d'épouvante
Dehors des hommes à chapeau claque se suivent à intervalle régulier
Pareils aux pluies que j'aimais
20   Alors qu'il faisait si beau
        « A la rage de Dieu » est le nom d'un cabaret où je suis entré
        hier
Il est écrit sur la devanture blanche en lettres plus pâles
Mais les femmes-marins qui glissent derrière les vitres
Sont trop heureuses pour être peureuses
25   Ici jamais de corps toujours l'assassinat sans preuves
Jamais le ciel toujours le silence
Jamais la liberté que pour la liberté

No Grounds

Art of days art of nights
The balance of bruises called Forgive
Red balance sensitive to the weight of a birdflight
When the snow-collared horsewomen with empty hands
5   Push their steam chariots upon the meadows
This balance incessantly berserk I see it
I see the ibis with the lovely manners
Returning from the pond laced into my heart
The wheels of dream charm the splendid furrows
10   Rising very high upon the shells of their costumes
And astonishment leaps here and there upon the sea
Go forth dear dawn forget nothing of my life
Take these roses climbing in the well of mirrors
Take the fluttering of all the lashes
15   Take even the threads holding up the steps of the ropewalkers and
     the drops of water
Art of days art of nights
I am at a window far off in a city full of dread
Outside men with crush hats succeed each other at regular intervals
Like the rains I used to love
20   When the weather was so fair
"The Wrath of God" is the name of a cabaret that I entered
     yesterday
It is written on the white façade in paler letters
But the sailor-women who glide behind the windows
Are too merry to be wary
25   Here never a body always the murder without proof
Never the sky always silence
Never freedom except for freedom

(MAC)

Le Verbe être

Je connais le désespoir dans ses grandes lignes. Le désespoir n'a pas d'ailes, il ne se tient pas nécessairement à une table desservie sur une terrasse, le soir, au bord de la mer. C'est le désespoir et ce n'est pas le retour d'une quantité de petits faits comme des graines qui quittent à la nuit tombante un sillon pour un autre. Ce n'est pas la mousse sur une pierre ou le verre à boire.[1] C'est un bateau criblé de neige, si vous voulez, comme les oiseaux qui tombent et leur sang n'a pas la moindre épaisseur. Je connais le désespoir dans ses grandes lignes. Une forme très petite, délimitée par des bijoux de cheveux. C'est le désespoir. Un collier de perles pour lequel on ne saurait trouver de fermoir et dont l'existence ne tient pas même à un fil, voilà le désespoir. Le reste nous n'en parlons pas. Nous n'avons pas fini de désespérer si nous commençons. Moi je désespère de l'abat-jour vers quatre heures, je désespère de l'éventail vers minuit, je désespère de la cigarette des condamnés. Je connais le désespoir dans ses grandes lignes. Le désespoir n'a pas de cœur, la main reste toujours au désespoir hors d'haleine, au désespoir dont les glaces ne nous disent jamais s'il est mort.[2] Je vis de ce désespoir qui m'enchante. J'aime cette mouche bleue qui vole dans le ciel à l'heure où les étoiles chantonnent. Je connais dans ses grandes lignes le désespoir aux longs étonnements[3] grêles, le désespoir de la fierté, le désespoir de la colère. Je me lève chaque jour comme tout le monde et je détends les bras sur un papier à fleurs, je ne me souviens de rien et c'est toujours avec désespoir que je découvre les beaux arbres déracinés de la nuit. L'air de la chambre est beau comme des baguettes de tambour. Il fait un temps de temps. Je connais le désespoir dans ses grandes lignes. C'est comme le vent du rideau qui me tend la perche. A-t-on idée d'un désespoir pareil! Au feu! Ah ils vont encore venir . . . Au secours! Les voici qui tombent dans l'escalier . . . Et les annonces de journal, et les réclames lumineuses le long du canal. Tas de sable, va, espèce de tas de sable! Dans ses grandes lignes le désespoir n'a pas d'importance. C'est une corvée d'arbres qui va encore faire une forêt, c'est une corvée d'étoiles qui va encore faire un jour de moins, c'est une corvée de jours de moins qui va encore faire ma vie.

The Verb To Be

I know despair in its broad outlines. Despair has no wings, it is not necessarily found at a cleared table upon a terrace, in the evening by the seaside. It is despair and it is not the return of a quantity of little facts like seeds leaving one furrow for another at nightfall. It is not moss upon a stone or a drinking glass.[1] It is a boat riddled with snow, if you please, like birds falling, and their blood has not the slightest thickness. I know despair in its broad outlines. A very small form, fringed by jewels of hair. It is despair. A necklace of pearls for which a clasp can never be found and whose existence does not hold even by a thread, that is despair. As for the rest, let's not speak of it. We haven't finished despairing if we begin. I myself despair of the lampshade around four o'clock, I despair of the fan around midnight, I despair of the condemned man's last cigarette. I know despair in its broad outlines. Despair has no heart, the hand always remains in despair out of breath, in despair whose death we are never told about by mirrors.[2] I live off this despair which so enchants me. I love that blue fly streaking in the sky at the hour when the stars hum their song. I know in its broad outlines despair with its long, slim breaches,[3] the despair of pride, the despair of anger. I rise every day like everyone and I stretch out my arms on a flowered wall-paper, I remember nothing and it is always with despair that I discover the lovely uprooted trees of the night. The air of the room is lovely like drumsticks. It is time weather. I know despair in its broad outlines. It is like the curtain wind giving me a helping hand. Can you imagine such despair: Fire, fire! Ah they are still going to come . . . Help! There they are falling down the stairs . . . And the newspaper advertisements, and the illuminated signs along the canal. Sandpile, go on with you, you old sandpile! In its broad outlines despair has no importance. It is a drudgery of trees that is going to make a forest again, a drudgery of stars that is going to make one less day again, a drudgery of days fewer which will again make up my life.

(MAC and MC)

La Forêt dans la hache

On vient de mourir mais je suis vivant et cependant je n'ai plus d'âme. Je n'ai plus qu'un corps transparent à l'intérieur duquel des colombes transparentes se jettent sur un poignard transparent tenu par une main transparente. Je vois l'effort dans toute sa beauté, l'effort réel qui ne se chiffre par rien, peu avant l'apparition de la dernière étoile. Le corps que j'habite comme une hutte et à forfait déteste l'âme que j'avais et qui surnage au loin. C'est l'heure d'en finir avec cette fameuse dualité qu'on m'a tant reprochée. Fini le temps où des yeux sans lumière et sans bagues puisaient le trouble dans les mares de la couleur. Il n'y a plus ni rouge ni bleu. Le rouge-bleu unanime s'efface à son tour comme un rouge-gorge dans les haies de l'inattention. On vient de mourir,—ni toi ni moi ni eux exactement mais nous tous, sauf moi qui survis de plusieurs façons: j'ai encore froid, par exemple. En voilà assez. Du feu! Du feu! Ou bien des pierres pour que je les fende, ou bien des oiseaux pour que je les suive, ou bien des corsets pour que je les serre autour de la taille des femmes mortes, et qu'elles ressuscitent, et qu'elles m'aiment, avec leurs cheveux fatigants, leurs regards défaits! Du feu, pour qu'on ne soit pas mort pour des prunes à l'eau-de-vie,[1] du feu pour que le chapeau de paille d'Italie[2] ne soit pas seulement une pièce de théâtre! Allo, le gazon! Allo, la pluie! C'est moi l'irréel souffle de ce jardin. La couronne noire posée sur ma tête est un cri de corbeaux migrateurs car il n'y avait jusqu'ici que des enterrés vivants, d'ailleurs en petit nombre, et voici que je suis le premier *aéré mort*.[3] Mais j'ai un corps pour ne plus m'en défaire, pour forcer les reptiles à m'admirer. Des mains sanglantes, des yeux de gui, une bouche de feuille morte et de verre (les feuilles mortes bougent sous le verre; elle ne sont pas aussi rouges qu'on le pense, quand l'indifférence expose ses méthodes voraces), des mains pour te cueillir, thym minuscule de mes rêves, romarin de mon extrême pâleur. Je n'ai plus d'ombre non plus. Ah mon ombre, ma chère ombre. Il faut que j'écrive une longue lettre à cette ombre que j'ai perdue. Je commencerai par Ma chère ombre. Ombre, ma chérie. Tu vois. Il n'y a plus de soleil. Il n'y a plus qu'un tropique sur deux. Il n'y a plus qu'un homme sur mille. Il n'y a plus qu'une femme sur l'absence de pensée qui caractérise en noir pur cette époque maudite. Cette femme tient un bouquet d'immortelles de la forme de mon sang.

The Forest in the Axe

Someone just died, but I'm alive and yet without a soul. I have nothing but a transparent body within which transparent doves fling themselves upon a transparent dagger held by a transparent hand. I see effort in all its beauty, real effort that cannot be measured by anything, just before the appearance of the last star. The body I inhabit like a hut and on lease detests the soul that I used to have and that stays afloat in the distance. The time has come to be done with this proverbial duality that has been blamed on me so much. Gone is the time when the turbulence in lightless and ringless eyes welled up from pools of color. There is neither red nor blue any longer. The unanimous red-blue fades out in turn like a robin redbreast in the hedges of neglect. Someone just died—neither you nor I exactly, nor they, but all of us, except for me who survives in many ways: for instance, I'm still cold. Enough of that. Fire! Fire! Or stones for me to cleave, or birds for me to follow, or corsets for me to lace tightly around dead women's waists, and so to make them come back to life and love me with their tiring hair and their chastened look! Fire, so we don't die for peanuts in the shell,[1] fire so the Italian straw hat[2] won't be just a play! Hello, lawn! Hello, rain! I'm the unreal breath of this garden. The black crown set on my head is a cry of migrating crows because until now there were only those buried alive, just a few of them, and now I'm the first of the *aired dead*.[3] But I have a body not to be done away with, to compel reptiles to admire me. Bloody hands, mistletoe eyes, a mouth of dead leaves and glass (the dead leaves stir underneath the glass; they aren't as red as you might think when indifference lays bare its voracious techniques), hands to gather you, minuscule thyme of my dreams, rosemary of my extreme pallor. I have no more shadow either. Ah, my shadow, dear shadow. I have to write a long letter to that now lost shadow. I'll begin by: My dear shadow. Shadow, my dearest. You see. There is no more sun. There is but one tropic out of two. No more than one man out of a thousand. No more than one woman out of the absence of thought which characterizes in pure black this damned age. That woman holds a bouquet of everlastings in the shape of my blood.

(MAC)

Toutes les écolières ensemble

Souvent tu dis marquant la terre du talon comme éclôt dans un
   buisson l'églantine
Sauvage qui n'a l'air faite que de rosée
Tu dis Toute la mer et tout le ciel pour une seule
Victoire d'enfance dans le pays de la danse ou mieux pour une seule
5   Etreinte dans le couloir d'un train
Qui va au diable avec les coups de fusil sur un pont ou mieux
Encore pour une seule farouche parole
Telle qu'en doit dire en vous regardant
Un homme sanglant dont le nom va très loin d'arbre en arbre
10 Qui ne fait qu'entrer et sortir parmi cent oiseaux de neige
Où donc est-ce bien
Et quand tu dis cela toute la mer et tout le ciel
S'éparpillent comme une nuée de petites filles dans la cour d'un
   pensionnat sévère
Après une dictée où *Le cœur m'en dit*
15 S'écrivait peut-être *Le cœur mendie*

All the Schoolgirls Together

Often you say making a mark in the earth with your heel as
    the wild rose blooms in a bush
Wild one seemingly made only of dew
You say The whole sea and the whole sky for a single
Victory of childhood in the country of dance or better for a single
5   Embrace in a train corridor
Going to the devil with rifle shots on a bridge or better
Yet for a single timorous word
Such as must be said while gazing at you
By a blood-stained man whose name goes far from tree to tree
10   Who keeps going in and out among a hundred birds of snow
Where then is it nice
And when you say it the whole sea and the whole sky
Scatter like a cloud of little girls in the yard of a strict boarding
    school
After a dictation in which *The heart takes*
15   Was perhaps written *The heart aches*

(JPC)

Nœud des miroirs

Les belles fenêtres ouvertes et fermées
Suspendues aux lèvres du jour
Les belles fenêtres en chemise
Les belles fenêtres aux cheveux de feu dans la nuit noire
5   Les belles fenêtres de cris d'alarme et de baisers
Au-dessus de moi au-dessous de moi derrière moi il y en a moins
        qu'en moi
Où elles ne font qu'un seul cristal[1] bleu comme les blés
Un diamant divisible en autant de diamants qu'il en faudrait pour se
        baigner à tous les bengalis
Et les saisons qui ne sont pas quatre mais quinze ou seize
10 En moi parmi lesquelles celle où le métal fleurit
Celle dont le sourire est moins qu'une dentelle
Celle où la rosée du soir unit les femmes et les pierres
Les saisons lumineuses comme l'intérieur d'une pomme dont on a
        détaché un quartier
Ou encore comme un quartier excentrique habité par des êtres qui
        sont de mèche avec le vent
15 Ou encore comme le vent de l'esprit qui la nuit ferre d'oiseaux sans
        bornes les chevaux à naseaux d'algèbre
Ou encore comme la formule[2]

Teinture de passiflore	{ aa 50 cent. cubes
Teinture d'aubépine	
Teinture de gui	5 cent. cubes
20 Teinture de scille	3 cent. cubes

        qui combat le bruit de galop

Les saisons remontent maille par maille leur filet brillant de l'eau
        vive de mes yeux

Knot of Mirrors

The lovely open and shut windows
Hanging on the lips of day
The lovely shirtclad windows
The lovely windows with fiery hair in the black night
5   The lovely windows of cries of alarm and of kisses
Above me below me behind me there are fewer than in me
Where they comprise but a single crystal[1] blue like stands of
    wheat
A diamond divisible into as many diamonds as would be necessary
    for all the waxbills to bathe in
And the seasons that are not four but fifteen or sixteen
10   In me among which the one when metal blooms
The one whose smile is less than lace
The one when the evening dew unites women and stones
Luminous seasons like the inside of an apple from which a quarter
    has been removed
Or else like an excentric quarter inhabited by beings who are in
    collusion with the wind
15   Or else like the wind of the spirit that shoes algebra-nostriled horses
at night with boundless birds
Or else like the formula[2]

Tincture of passion flower
Tincture of hawthorn   { aa 50 cubic cent.
Tincture of mistletoe   5 cubic cent.
20   Tincture of squill   3 cubic cent.

that fights the sound of galloping

The seasons raise up mesh by mesh their brilliant net from the
    spring water of my eyes

Et dans ce filet il y a ce que j'ai vu c'est la spire d'un fabuleux
coquillage
Qui me rappelle l'exécution en vase clos de l'empereur
Maximilien
25   Il y a ce que j'ai aimé c'est le plus haut rameau de l'arbre de corail qui
sera foudroyé
C'est le *style* du cadran solaire à minuit vrai
Il y a ce que je connais bien ce que je connais si peu que prête-moi
tes serres vieux délire
Pour m'élever avec mon cœur le long de la cataracte
Les aéronautes parlent de l'efflorescence de l'air en hiver

And in this net there is what I saw it's the whorl of a fabulous shell
That reminds me of the execution in an airtight chamber of the
    emperor Maximilian
25   There is what I loved it's the highest limb of the coral tree that will
    be blasted by lightning
It's the *style* of the sundial at true midnight
There is what I know well what I know so little that lend me your
    claws old delirium
To lift me with my heart along the waterfall
Aeronauts speak of the efflorescence of air in winter

(JPC)

Facteur Cheval[I]

Nous les oiseaux que tu charmes toujours du haut de ces belvédères
Et qui chaque nuit ne faisons qu'une branche fleurie de tes épaules
    aux bras de ta brouette bien-aimée
Qui nous arrachons plus vifs que des étincelles à ton poignet
Nous sommes les soupirs de la statue de verre qui se soulève sur le
    coude quand l'homme dort
5   Et que des brèches brillantes s'ouvrent dans son lit
Brèches par lesquelles on peut apercevoir des cerfs aux bois de corail
    dans une clairière
Et des femmes nues tout au fond d'une mine
Tu t'en souviens tu te levais alors tu descendais du train
Sans un regard pour la locomotive en proie aux immenses racines
    barométriques
10   Qui se plaint dans la forêt vierge de toutes ses chaudières meurtries
Ses cheminées fumant de jacinthes et mue par des serpents bleus[2]
Nous te précédions alors nous les plantes sujettes à métamorphoses
Qui chaque nuit nous faisons des signes que l'homme peut
    surprendre
Tandis que sa maison s'écroule et qu'il s'étonne devant les
    emboîtements singuliers
15   Que recherche son lit avec le corridor et l'escalier
L'escalier se ramifie indéfiniment
Il mène à une porte de meule il s'élargit tout à coup sur une place
    publique
Il est fait de dos de cygnes une aile ouverte pour la rampe
Il tourne sur lui-même comme s'il allait se mordre
20   Mais non il se contente sur nos pas d'ouvrir toutes ses marches
    comme des tiroirs
Tiroirs de pain tiroirs de vin tiroirs de savon tiroirs de glaces tiroirs
    d'escaliers
Tiroirs de chair à la poignée de cheveux
A cette heure où des milliers de canards de Vaucanson[3] se lissent les
    plumes
Sans te retourner tu saisissais la truelle dont on fait les seins

Postman Cheval[I]

We the birds that you always charm from atop those lookouts
And who each night merge into a single flowering branch from your
    shoulders to the arms of your beloved wheelbarrow
Who tear ourselves away from your wrist more vividly than sparks
We are the sighs of the glass statue that raises itself on its elbow
    when man sleeps
5   And may glowing gaps open up in his bed
Gaps through which can be glimpsed stags with coral antlers in a
    clearing
And naked women at the very bottom of a mine
You remember you would arise then you would step off the train
Without a glance at the locomotive preyed upon by immense
    barometric roots
10   That cries out dolefully in the virgin forest with all of its mauled
    boilers
Its stacks puffing hyacinths and propelled by blue serpents[2]
We would then move ahead of you we the plants prone to
    metamorphoses
Who each night send signals to ourselves that man can pick up
While his house collapses and he wonders at the odd
    interconnections
15   That his bed seeks with the hallway and the staircase
The staircase branches out indefinitely
It leads to a millstone door it widens suddenly onto a public square
It is made of swan backs with one wing extended as a railing
It spins upon itself as if to bite itself
20   But no it is content as we advance to open all its steps like drawers
Bread drawers wine drawers soap drawers mirror drawers staircase
    drawers
Flesh drawers with handles of hair
At the moment when thousands of Vaucanson[3] ducks preen their
    feathers
Without looking back you would grab the trowel that breasts are
    made of

25   Nous te souriions tu nous tenais par la taille
     Et nous prenions les attitudes de ton plaisir
     Immobiles sous nos paupières pour toujours comme la femme aime
          voir l'homme
     Après avoir fait l'amour

25 We would smile at you you held us by the waist
And we would take on the configurations of your pleasure
Motionless beneath our eyelids forever as a woman loves to see a
   man
After making love

(JPC)

Rideau rideau

Les théâtres vagabonds des saisons qui auront joué ma vie
Sous mes sifflets
L'avant-scène avait été aménagée en cachot d'où je pouvais siffler[1]
Les mains aux barreaux je voyais sur fond de verdure noire
5   L'héroïne nue jusqu'à la ceinture
Qui se suicidait au début du premier acte
La pièce se poursuivait inexplicablement dans le lustre
La scène se couvrant peu à peu de brouillard
Et je criais parfois
10   Je brisais la cruche qu'on m'avait donnée et de laquelle s'échappaient
      des papillons
Qui montaient follement vers le lustre
Sous prétexte d'intermède encore de ballet qu'on tenait à me donner
      de mes pensées
J'essayais alors de m'ouvrir le poignet avec les morceaux de terre
      brune
Mais c'étaient des pays dans lesquels je m'étais perdu
15   Impossible de retrouver le fil de ces voyages
J'étais séparé de tout par le pain du soleil
Un personnage circulait dans la salle seul personnage agile
Qui s'était fait un masque de mes traits
Il prenait odieusement parti pour l'ingénue et pour le traître
20   Le bruit courait que c'était arrangé comme mai juin juillet août
Soudain la caverne se faisait plus profonde
Dans les couloirs interminables des bouquets tenus à hauteur de
      main
Erraient seuls c'est à peine si j'osais entrouvrir ma porte
Trop de liberté m'était accordée à la fois
25   Liberté de m'enfuir en traîneau de mon lit
Liberté de faire revivre les êtres qui me manquent

Curtain Curtain

The vagabond theatres of the seasons which will have played out my
    life
Under my catcalls
The forestage had been set up as a cell from which I could hiss[1]
My hands on the bars I could see against a backdrop of dark
    greenery
5   The heroine bare to the waist
Committing suicide at the beginning of the first act
The play went on inexplicably in the chandelier
The stage gradually clouding over
And sometimes I shouted
10 I broke the jug they had given me and from which butterflies escaped
Rising crazily toward the chandelier
Under pretense of an interlude they insisted on presenting me a
    ballet of my thoughts
I then tried to slash my wrist with clods of dark earth
But they were countries where I had lost my way
15 Impossible to recapture the thread of these travels
I was separated from everything by the round loaf of the sun
A character moved about the hall the only agile one
Who had made himself a mask with my features
He viciously sided with the ingenue and the traitor
20 Rumors spread that it was arranged like May June July August
Suddenly the cavern became deeper
In the endless corridors bouquets held at hand level
Were wandering alone I hardly dared to open my door a crack
Too much freedom was granted me at once
25 Freedom to escape in a sleigh from my bed
Freedom to bring back to life the persons I miss

Les chaises d'aluminium se resserraient autour d'un kiosque de
glaces[2]
Sur lequel se levait un rideau de rosée frangé de sang devenu vert
Liberté de chasser devant moi les apparences réelles

30   Le sous-sol était merveilleux sur un mur blanc apparaissait en
pointillé de feu ma silhouette percée au cœur d'une balle

The aluminum chairs drew closer together around a kiosk of
    mirrors[2]
On which a curtain of dew arose fringed with blood turned green
Freedom to chase real appearances before me
30   The basement was marvelous there appeared on a white wall
    my silhouette fire-specked and pierced with a bullet in my heart

(MAC)

Le Sphinx vertébral

La belle ombre patiente et courbe fait le tour des pavés
Les fenêtres vénitiennes s'ouvrent et se ferment sur la place
Où vont en liberté des bêtes suivies de feux
Les réverbères mouillés bruissent encadrés d'une nuée d'yeux bleus
5 Qui couvrent le paysage en amont de la ville
Ce matin proue du soleil comme tu t'engloutis dans les superbes
      chants exhalés à l'ancienne derrière les rideaux par les guetteuses
      nues
Tandis que les arums géants tournent autour de leur taille
Et que le mannequin sanglant saute sur ses trois pieds dans le
      grenier
Il vient disent-elles en cambrant leur cou sur lequel le bondissement
      des nattes libère des glaciers à peine roses
10 Qui se fendent sous le poids d'un rai de lumière tombant des
      persiennes arrachées
Il vient c'est le loup aux dents de verre
Celui qui mange l'heure dans les petites boîtes rondes
Celui qui souffle les parfums trop pénétrants des herbes
Celui qui fume les petits feux de passage le soir dans les navets
15 Les colonnes des grands appartements de marbre et de vétiver crient
Elles crient elles sont prises de ces mouvements de va-et-vient qui
      n'animaient jusque-là que certaines pièces colossales des usines
Les femmes immobiles sur les plaques tournantes vont voir
Il fait jour à gauche mais nuit complètement nuit à droite
Il y a des branchages encore pleins d'oiseaux qui passent à toute
      allure obscurcissant le trou de la croisée
20 Des oiseaux blancs qui pondent des œufs noirs
Où sont ces oiseaux que remplacent maintenant des étoiles bordées
      de deux rangs de perles
Une tête de poisson très très longue ce n'est pas encore lui
De la tête de poisson naissent des jeunes filles secouant un tamis
Et du tamis des cœurs faits de larmes bataviques[1]

The Vertebral Sphinx

Patient and curved the lovely shadow walks round the paving stones
The Venetian windows open and close upon the square
Where beasts move freely fires trailing
Wet streetlamps rustle in a frame of swarming blue eyes
5   That cover the landscape upstream from the town
This morning prow of the sun how you steep yourself in the superb
      songs sighed in a traditional mode behind the curtains by the
      naked women keeping watch
While the giant arum lilies turn about their waist
The bloody mannequin hopping on all three feet in the attic
He's coming they say arching their necks where the bounce of braids
      sets free faintly pink glaciers
10   That split under the weight of a ray of light falling from the torn-off
      blinds
He's coming it's the glass-toothed wolf
Who eats up time in little round boxes
Who blows the overpungent fragrances of herbs
Who smokes little guide fires in the turnips at evening
15   The columns of the great apartments of marble and vetiver cry out
They cry caught in those to-and-fro motions which until then
      enlivened only certain colossal castings in factories
The motionless women on turntables will see
There is daylight on the left but night has completely fallen on the
      right
There are branches still full of birds that darken the gap in the
      casement window as they speed by
20   White birds laying black eggs
Where are those birds replaced now by stars edged with twin strands
      of pearls
A very very long fish head it is not yet he
From the fish head girls are born shaking a sieve
And from the sieve hearts made of Prince Rupert's drops[1]

25   II vient c'est le loup aux dents de verre
      Celui qui volait très haut sur les terrains vagues reparus au-dessus
          des maisons
      Avec des plantes aiguisées toutes tournées vers ses yeux
      D'un vert à défier une bouteille de mousse renversée sur la neige
      Ses griffes de jade dans lesquelles il se mire en volant
30   Son poil de la couleur des étincelles
      C'est lui qui gronde dans les forges au crépuscule et dans les lingeries
          abandonnées
      Il est visible on le touche il avance avec son balancier[2] sur le fil tendu
          d'hirondelles
      Les guetteuses se penchent se penchent aux fenêtres
      De tout leur côté d'ombre de tout leur côté de lumière
35   La bobine du jour est tirée par petits coups du côté du paradis de
          sable
      Les pédales de la nuit bougent sans interruption

25   He's coming it's the glass-toothed wolf
Who was flying high above the vacant sites that reappeared above
    the houses
With sharp-leaved plants turned toward his eyes
Of such a green as to challenge a bottle of moss spilled upon the
    snow
His jade talons in which he gazes admiringly at himself while in flight
30   His fur the color of sparks
It is he who growls in the forges at dusk and in deserted
    linen-rooms
Visible he can be touched moving forward with his balancing-pole[2]
    over the swallow-lined wire
The watchful women lean out lean out of the windows
With their whole shadow side their whole side of light
35   The bobbin of day is tugged bit by bit toward the side of the sand
    paradise
The treadles of night move ceaselessly

(MAC)

Vigilance

A Paris la tour Saint-Jacques[1] chancelante
Pareille à un tournesol
Du front vient quelquefois heurter la Seine et son ombre glisse
    imperceptiblement parmi les remorqueurs
A ce moment sur la pointe des pieds dans mon sommeil
5   Je me dirige vers la chambre où je suis étendu
Et j'y mets le feu
Pour que rien ne subsiste de ce consentement qu'on m'a arraché
Les meubles font alors place à des animaux de même taille qui me
    regardent fraternellement
Lions dans les crinières desquels achèvent de se consumer les chaises
10   Squales dont le ventre blanc s'incorpore le dernier frisson des draps
A l'heure de l'amour et des paupières bleues
Je me vois brûler à mon tour je vois cette cachette solennelle de riens
Qui fut mon corps
Fouillée par les becs patients des ibis du feu
15   Lorsque tout est fini j'entre invisible dans l'arche
Sans prendre garde aux passants de la vie qui font sonner très loin
    leurs pas traînants
Je vois les arêtes du soleil
A travers l'aubépine de la pluie
J'entends se déchirer le linge humain comme une grande feuille
20   Sous l'ongle de l'absence et de la présence qui sont de connivence
Tous les métiers se fanent il ne reste d'eux qu'une dentelle parfumée
Une coquille de dentelle qui a la forme parfaite d'un sein
Je ne touche plus que le cœur des choses je tiens le fil

Vigilance

In Paris, the Tour Saint-Jacques[1]
Swaying like a sunflower
Sometimes against the Seine its shadow moves among the tugboats
Just then on tiptoe in my sleep
5   I go toward the room where I am lying
And set it afire
Nothing remains of the consent I had to give
The furniture then makes way for the beasts looking at me like
    brothers
Lions whose manes consume the chairs
10 Sharks' white bellies absorb the sheets' last quiver
At the hour of love and blue eyelids
I see myself burning now I see the solemn hiding place of nothings
Which was once my body
Probed by the patient beaks firebirds
15 When all is finished I enter the ark unseen
Taking no heed of life's passerby whose shuffling steps are heard far
    off
I see the ridges of the sun
Through the hawthorn of the rain
I hear human linen tearing like a great leaf
20 Under the fingernails of absence and presence in collusion
All the looms are withering just a bit of perfumed lace
A shell of lace remains in a perfect breast shape
I touch nothing but the heart of things I hold the thread

(MAC)

Sans connaissance[I]

On n'a pas oublié
La singulière tentative d'enlèvement
Tiens une étoile pourtant il fait encore grand jour
De cette jeune fille de quatorze ans
5   Quatre de plus que de doigts
Qui regagnait en ascenseur
Je vois ses seins comme si elle était nue
On dirait des mouchoirs séchant sur un rosier
L'appartement de ses parents
10   Le père un piquet solidement enfoncé dans l'ombre la mère jolie
      pyramide d'abat-jour
Appartement situé au quatrième étage d'un immeuble de la rue
      Saint-Martin
Non loin de la Porte[2] gardée par deux salamandres géantes
Sous laquelle je me tiens moi-même plusieurs heures par jour
Que je sois à Paris ou non
15   La belle Euphorbe appelons la jeune fille Euphorbe
S'inquiète de l'arrêt de l'ascenseur entre le deuxième et le troisième
      étage
A six heures du soir quand le quartier Saint-Martin commence à
      broyer de la craie[3] du plantain du vitrail
Rester ainsi suspendue comme une aiguillette à une veste mexicaine
N'a rien de particulièrement réjouissant
20   Le palier du second à quelques pieds au-dessous d'Euphorbe charrie
      des planches claires l'anguille d'une rampe et quelques jolies
      herbes noires très longues
Qui ressemblent à un vêtement d'homme
La jeune fille surprise en pleine ascension se compare à un diabolo
      de plumes
Elle a les yeux plus verts que d'ordinaire n'est verte l'angélique
Et ces yeux plongent se brûlent à d'autres yeux sur lesquels glisse une
      flamme de bore[4]

Unconscious[1]

One has not forgotten
The odd attempted abduction
Hey a star and yet it's still broad daylight
Of that fourteen-year-old girl
5   Four more years than fingers
Who was returning in an elevator
I see her breasts as if she were naked
They look like handkerchiefs drying on a rosebush
To her parents' apartment
10   The father a post firmly set in the shadows the mother a pretty
      lampshade pyramid
An apartment located on the fourth floor of a building in the rue
      Saint-Martin
Not far from the Porte[2] guarded by two giant salamanders
Under which I stand several hours a day
Whether I am in Paris or not
15   The lovely Euphorbe let us call the girl Euphorbe
Is concerned about the elevator stopping between the third and
      fourth floors
At 6:00 P.M. when the Saint-Martin quarter starts pounding chalk[3]
      plantain stained glass
To remain thus suspended like an aiguillette on a Mexican jacket
Is by no means particularly amusing
20   The third floor landing a few feet below Euphorbe carries adrift
      light-colored boards the eel of a hand-rail and a few very long
      pretty blades of black grass
Resembling a man's clothing
The girl surprised in full ascent compares herself to a feathered
      jack-in-the-box
She has greener eyes than angelica green usually is
And her eyes look down deep are scorched by other eyes across
      which a boron flame[4] flitters

25 D'en bas les mollets d'Euphorbe luisent un peu de biais ce sont deux
   oiseaux sombres qui doivent être plus tièdes et plus doux que tous
   les autres
   Les yeux de bore s'y fixent un instant puis le regard étincelant s'évase
   dans la robe
   Très fine qui est de Paris
   C'en est assez pour que ces deux êtres se soient compris
   Ainsi dans une hutte par temps de pluie sous les tropiques
   l'énervement fait merveille
30 Les insectes à taille minuscule déployant de véritables drapeaux qui
   traînent partout dans les coins
   Une porte qui glisse sur elle-même avec le bruit d'une ombrelle
   qu'on ferme
   L'enfant est dans les bras de l'homme il sent frémir la chair au-dessus
   des jarrets sous la robe qui remonte un peu comme un fuchsia
   L'escalier mal éclairé des ombres grandissent sur le mur de faux
   marbre chair
   Ombres de chevaux lancés à toutes guides dans la tempête
35 Ombres de buissons qui courent à leur tour largement dépassés
   Et surtout ombres de danseurs toujours le même couple sur une
   plaque tournante bordée de draps
   Cet instant fait dérailler le train rond des pendules
   La rue jette des éclairs Euphorbe sourit sournoisement entre la
   crainte et le plaisir
   Je vois son cœur à cette minute il est distrait coupant il est le
   premier bourgeon qui saute d'un marronnier rose
40 Un mot et tout est sauvé
   Un mot et tout est perdu
   L'inconnu là la tentation comme nulle part ailleurs sous ce ciel à la
   paille de fer
   Mais aussi la peur sous cette voûte affolante de pas qui vont et qui
   viennent
   A faire un amas de plâtre de cette maison qui est bien loin
45 Un amas de plâtre dans un abri duquel on commencerait à s'aimer
   La peur à oublier ses doigts dans un livre pour ne plus
   toucher

25   From below seen slightly askance Euphorbe's calves glisten they
       are two dark birds that must be warmer and softer than all
       the others
     The boron eyes linger on them for a moment then the flashing gaze
       tapers into the dress
     A very fine one from Paris
     That is enough for these two creatures to understand each other
     Thus in a hut under rainy skies in the tropics excitement works
       wonders
30   Tiny-waisted insects unfurling real flags that lie about everywhere in
       nooks and corners
     A door sliding down on itself with the noise of a parasol being shut
     The child is in the man's arms he feels her flesh quivering above the
       knees under the dress that rises up a little like a fuchsia
     Poorly lit stairs shadows expand against the wall of false marble
       flesh
     Shadows of horses flung at full rein into the storm
35   Shadows of running bushes outdistanced in turn
     And especially shadows of dancers always the same couple on a
       turntable edged with sheets
     That instant derails the clocks' round train
     The street emits flashes of lightning Euphorbe smiles slyly between
       fear and pleasure
     I see her heart at this minute it's distracted cutting it's the first bud
       leaping from a pink chestnut tree
40   One word and all is saved
     One word and all is lost
     The stranger there temptation like nowhere else under that sky of
       iron shavings
     But also fear under this archway frantic with steps that come
       and go
     Such as to make a mound of plaster of this house which is far away
45   A mound of plaster within whose shelter one would start loving
     Such fear as to forget one's fingers in a book in order to touch no
       more

A fermer ses yeux dans le sillage du premier venu pour éperdument
le fuir
Quelle seconde
On sait le reste
50   Pfuût houch le coup de revolver le sang qui saute lestement les
marches vertes
Pas assez vite pour que l'homme
Son signalement 1 m. 65 la concierge n'a pas osé arrêter ce visiteur
inhabituel mais poli
Il était d'autre part très bien de sa personne
Ne s'éloigne en allumant une cigarette[5]
55   Plus douce que la douleur d'aimer et d'être aimé

As to shut one's eyes in the wake of a chance encounter in order to
   flee desperately from that person
What a second
The rest is known
50   Pfft whoosh the pistol shot blood leaping nimbly down the green
   steps
Not fast enough to prevent the man
His description 1.65 meters tall the concierge didn't dare stop this
   unusual but polite visitor
Besides he cut a very dashing figure
From moving away lighting a cigarette[5]
55   Sweeter than the pain of loving and being loved

(JPC)

Une Branche d'ortie entre
par la fenêtre

La femme au corps de papier peint
La tanche[1] rouge des cheminées
Dont la mémoire est faite d'une multitude de petits abreuvoirs
Pour les navires au loin
5   Et qui rit comme un peu de braise qu'on aurait enchâssée dans la
       neige
Et qui se voit grandir et diminuer la nuit sur des pas d'accordéon
La cuirasse des herbes la poignée de la porte des poignards
Celle qui descend des paillettes du sphinx
Celle qui met des roulettes au fauteuil du Danube
10 Celle pour qui l'espace et le temps se déchirent le soir quand le
       veilleur de son œil vacille comme un elfe
N'est pas l'enjeu du combat que se livrent mes rêves
Oiseau cassant
Que la nature tend sur les fils télégraphiques des transes
Et qui chavire sur le grand lac de nombres de son chant
15 Elle est le double cœur de la muraille perdue
A laquelle s'agrippent les sauterelles du sang
Qui traînent mon apparence de miroir mes mains de faille
Mes yeux de chenilles mes cheveux de longues baleines noires
De baleines cachetées d'une cire étincelante et noire

A Stalk of Nettle Enters
through the Window

The woman with the wallpaper body
The red tench[1] of chimneys
Whose memory is made up of a multitude of small drinking troughs
For faraway ships
5   And who laughs like an ember as if it were inlaid in snow
And who is seen to grow and decrease at night on accordion steps
The armor of grass the knob of the daggers' door
She who descends from the spangles of the sphinx
She who puts rollers on the Danube's chair
10   She for whose sake space and time are torn in the evening when the
      watchman with his eye totters like an elf
Is not at stake in the battle fought by my dreams
Brittle bird
That nature stretches out on the telegraph wires of trances
And who capsizes into the great lake of numbers of her song
15   She is the double heart of the lost wall
To which the blood's grasshoppers cling
That drag my mirror-like appearance my faille hands
My caterpillar eyes my long black whalebone hair
Whalebone sealed under a glittering black wax

(JPC)

Le Grand Secours meurtrier

La statue de Lautréamont[1]
Au socle de cachets de quinine
En rase campagne
L'auteur des Poésies est couché à plat ventre
5   Et près de lui veille l'héloderme[2] suspect
Son oreille gauche appliquée au sol est une boîte vitrée
Occupée par un éclair l'artiste n'a pas oublié de faire figurer au-
    dessus de lui
Le ballon bleu ciel en forme de tête de Turc
Le cygne de Montevideo[3] dont les ailes sont déployées et toujours
    prêtes à battre
10   Lorsqu'il s'agit d'attirer de l'horizon les autres cygnes
Ouvre sur le faux univers deux yeux de couleurs différentes
L'un de sulfate de fer sur la treille des cils l'autre de boue diamantée
Il voit le grand hexagone à entonnoir dans lequel se crisperont
    bientôt les machines
Que l'homme s'acharne à couvrir de pansements
15   Il ravive de sa bougie de radium les fonds du creuset humain
Le sexe de plumes le cerveau de papier huilé
Il préside aux cérémonies deux fois nocturnes qui ont pour but
    soustraction faite du feu d'intervertir les cœurs de l'homme et de
    l'oiseau
J'ai accès près de lui en qualité de convulsionnaire[4]
Les femmes ravissantes qui m'introduisent dans le wagon capitonné
    de roses
20   Où un hamac qu'elles ont pris soin de me faire de leurs chevelures
    m'est réservé
De toute éternité
Me recommandent avant de partir de ne pas prendre froid dans la
    lecture du journal
Il paraît que la statue près de laquelle le chiendent[5] de mes terminai-
    sons nerveuses
Arrive à destination est accordée chaque nuit comme un piano

Deadly Rescue

Lautréamont's statue[1]
With its base of quinine tablets
In the open country
The author of the Poems is lying face down
5   And near him the heloderm[2] watches under suspicion
His left ear to the ground is a glassed-in box
Filled by a flash the artist did not forget to have represented above
    him
The sky-blue balloon in the shape of a turban top
The swan of Montevideo[3] whose wings are spread out and always
    ready to flap
10   When there arises a need to attract the other swans from the horizon
Opens upon the false universe two eyes of different colors
One of iron sulfate on an eyelash trellis the other of diamond-
    studded mud
He sees the great cratered hexagon in which machines will soon
    flinch
Which man strives to cover with bandages
15   He rekindles with his radium candle the depths of the human
    crucible
The sex of feathers the brain of oiled paper
He presides over doubly nocturnal ceremonies whose goal fire
    notwithstanding is to interchange the hearts of man and bird
As a convulsionary[4] I have close access to him
The lovely women who usher me into the railway car upholstered
    with roses
20   Where a hammock that they have taken the trouble to make with
    their tresses is set aside for me
For all eternity
Advise me before leaving not to catch a cold in reading the
    newspaper
It seems that the statue near which the wormwood[5] of my nerve
    endings
Arrives at its destination is tuned every night like a piano

(JPC)

From *L'Air de l'eau* [Airwater]

1934

Monde dans un baiser
Le joueur à baguettes de coudrier cousues sur les manches
Apaise un essaim de jeunes singes-lions
Descendus à grand fracas de la corniche
5   Tout devient opaque je vois passer le carrosse de la nuit
Traîné par les axolotls[1] à souliers bleus
Entrée scintillante de la voie de fait[2] qui mène au tombeau
Pavé de paupières avec leurs cils
La loi du talion use un peuple d'étoiles
10   Et tu te diapres pour moi d'une rosée noire
Tandis que les effrayantes bornes mentales
A cheveux de vigne
Se fendent dans le sens de la longueur
Livrant passage à des aigrettes
15   Qui regagnent le lac voisin
Les barreaux du spectacle sont merveilleusement tordus
Un long fuseau d'air atteste seul la fuite de l'homme.
Au petit matin dans les luzernes illustres
L'heure
20   N'est plus que ce que sonnent les pièces d'or de la bohémienne
Aux volants de coréopsis[3]
Une écuyère debout sur un cheval au galop pommelé de boules
    d'orage
De loin les bras sont toujours en extension latérale
Le losange poudreux du dessous me rappelle
25   La tente décorée de bisons bleus
Par les Indiens de l'oreiller[4]
Dehors l'air essaye les gants de gui
Sur un comptoir d'eau pure
Monde dans un baiser monde
30   A moi les écailles
Les écailles de la grande tortue céleste à ventre d'hydrophile[5]
Qui se bat chaque nuit dans l'amour
Avec la grande tortue noire le gigantesque scolopendre[6] de racines

World in a kiss
The player of hazel dowsing rods sewn on the sleeves
Appeases a swarm of young lion-monkeys
Descended in a hubbub from the ledge

5   All becomes opaque I see the carriage of night passing
Drawn by the axolotls¹ in blue shoes
Sparkling entry of the path of violence² leading to the tomb
Paved with eyelids and their lashes
The law of retaliation wears down a people of stars

10   And you take on for me a hue of dark dew
While the fearful mental curbs
With vine hair
Cleave lengthwise
Making way for egrets

15   Returning to the nearby lake
The rails of the spectacle are marvelously twisted
A long air spindle alone bears witness to the flight of man
At daybreak in the fabulous alfalfa
The time

20   Is now no more than what is rung by the gold pieces of the bohemian
With coreopsis³ flounces
A horsewoman standing on a galloping steed dappled with
     stormballs
From far off the arms are still extended laterally
The powdery lozenge beneath reminds me

25   Of the tent decorated with blue buffaloes
By the pillow Indians⁴
Outside the air tries on mistletoe gloves
On a counter of pure water
World in a kiss world

30   Mine is the shell
The shell of the great celestial tortoise with its hydrophilus⁵ stomach
Struggling each night in love
With the great black tortoise the gigantic centipede⁶ of roots

(MAC)

Je rêve je te vois superposée indéfiniment à toi-même
Tu es assise sur le haut tabouret de corail
Devant ton miroir toujours à son premier quartier
Deux doigts sur l'aile d'eau du peigne
5   Et en même temps
Tu reviens de voyage tu t'attardes la dernière dans la grotte
Ruisselante d'éclairs
Tu ne me reconnais pas
Tu es étendue sur le lit tu t'éveilles ou tu t'endors
10   Tu t'éveilles où tu t'es endormie ou ailleurs
Tu es nue la balle de sureau rebondit encore
Mille balles de sureau bourdonnent au-dessus de toi
Si légères qu'à chaque instant ignorées de toi
Ton souffle ton sang sauvés de la folle jonglerie de l'air
15   Tu traverses la rue les voitures lancées sur toi ne sont plus que
      leur ombre
Et la même
Enfant
Prise dans un soufflet de paillettes
Tu sautes à la corde
20   Assez longtemps pour qu'apparaisse au haut de l'escalier invisible
Le seul papillon vert qui hante les sommets de l'Asie
Je caresse tout ce qui fut toi
Dans tout ce qui doit l'être encore
J'écoute siffler mélodieusement
25   Tes bras innombrables
Serpent unique dans tous les arbres
Tes bras au centre desquels tourne le cristal de la rose des vents[1]
Ma fontaine vivante de Sivas[2]

◀

I dream I see your image indefinitely imposed upon itself
You are seated on the high coral stool
Before your mirror still in its first quarter
Two fingers on the water wing of your comb
5   And at the same time
You are returning from a trip lingering last in the grotto
Streaming with sparks
You do not recognize me
You are lying on the bed you wake or you fall asleep
10   You wake where you fell asleep or elsewhere
You are naked the elderberry still bounces
A thousand elderberries buzz above you
So light that at every moment unbeknownst to you
Your breath your blood saved from the air's mad juggling
15   You cross the street the cars that rush at you turn to a shadow
And the same
Child
Caught in a bellows of spangles
You are skipping rope
20   Until atop the unseen stairs appears
The sole green butterfly that haunts the Asian peaks
I caress all that you were
In all that you still will be
I hear your countless arms
25   Whistle tunefully
Snake unique in all the trees
In your arms turn the crystal rose of winds[1]
My living fountain of Shiva[2]

(MAC)

Le marquis de Sade a regagné l'intérieur du volcan en éruption
D'où il était venu
Avec ses belles mains encore frangées
Ses yeux de jeune fille
5   Et cette raison à fleur de sauve-qui-peut qui ne fut
Qu'à lui
Mais du salon phosphorescent à lampes de viscères
Il n'a cessé de jeter les ordres mystérieux
Qui ouvrent une brèche dans la nuit morale
10   C'est par cette brèche que je vois
Les grandes ombres craquantes la vieille écorce minée
Se dissoudre
Pour me permettre de t'aimer
Comme le premier homme aima la première femme
15   En toute liberté
Cette liberté
Pour laquelle le feu même s'est fait homme
Pour laquelle le marquis de Sade défia les siècles de ses grands arbres
        abstraits
D'acrobates tragiques
20   Cramponnés au fil de la Vierge[I] du désir

The Marquis de Sade has gone back inside the erupting volcano
From which he had come
With his lovely hands still fringed
His young girl's eyes
5   And that rationality on the edge of hurry-scurry which was
His alone
But from the phosphorescent salon with viscera lamps
He has not stopped letting fly those mysterious commands
That break through the moral night
10 Through that breach I can see
The great cracking shadows the old undermined bark
Dissolving
To permit my loving you
As the first man loved the first woman
15 In total freedom
That freedom
For which fire itself became man
For which the Marquis de Sade defied the centuries with his great
        abstract trees
Of tragic acrobats
20 Clutching the gossamer[1] of desire

(MAC)

Au beau demi-jour

Au beau demi-jour de 1934
L'air était une splendide rose couleur de rouget
Et la forêt quand je me préparais à y entrer
Commençait par un arbre à feuilles de papier à cigarettes
5   Parce que je t'attendais
Et que si tu te promènes avec moi
N'importe où
Ta bouche est volontiers la nielle
D'où repart sans cesse la roue bleue diffuse et brisée qui monte
10   Blêmir dans l'ornière
Tous les prestiges se hâtaient à ma rencontre
Un écureuil était venu appliquer son ventre blanc sur mon cœur
Je ne sais comment il se tenait
Mais la terre était pleine de reflets plus profonds que ceux de l'eau
15   Comme si le métal eût enfin secoué sa coque
Et toi couchée l'effroyable mer de pierreries
Tu tournais
Nue
Dans un grand soleil de feu d'artifice
20   Je te voyais descendre lentement des radiolaires
Les coquilles même de l'oursin j'y étais
Pardon je n'y étais déjà plus
J'avais levé la tête car le vivant écrin de velours blanc m'avait quitté
Et j'étais triste
25   Le ciel entre les feuilles luisait hagard et dur comme une libellule
J'allais fermer les yeux
Quand les deux pans du bois qui s'étaient brusquement écartés
     s'abattirent
Sans bruit
Comme les deux feuilles centrales d'un muguet immense

In the lovely twilight

In the lovely twilight of 1934
The air was a splendid red mullet rose
And the forest I was about to enter
Began by a tree with cigarette paper leaves
5   Because I was awaiting you
And when you walk with me
No matter where
The blue wheel diffuse and broken starts off from
Your corncockle mouth to rise
10   And turn pale in the rut
All the marvels rushed to meet me
A squirrel had come to touch its white stomach to my heart
I don't know how he held there
But the earth was full of reflections deeper than the water's
15   As if the metal had finally shaken off its shell
And you lying on the frightening sea of gemstones
You were turning
Naked
In a great sun of fireworks
20   I saw you slowly descend from the radiolaria
Even in the sea urchin shells I was there
Forgive me I was there no longer
I had raised my head for the living sheath of white velvet had left
     me
And I was sad
25   The sky between the leaves shone haggard and harsh like a dragonfly
I was going to close my eyes
When the two wood panels pulled apart and fell
Without noise
Like the two central leaves of a great lily of the valley

30   D'une fleur capable de contenir toute la nuit
      J'étais où tu me vois
      Dans le parfum sonné à toute volée
      Avant qu'elles ne revinssent comme chaque jour à la vie changeante
      J'eus le temps de poser mes lèvres
35   Sur tes cuisses de verre

30   A flower able to contain the whole night
     I was where you see me
     In the perfume sounded in full peal
     Before they came back to the daily ebb and flow of life
     I had time to place my lips
35   On your thighs of glass

(MAC)

Yeux zinzolins

Yeux zinzolins[1] de la petite Babylonienne trop blanche
Au nombril sertissant une pierre de même couleur
Quand s'ouvre comme une croisée sur un jardin nocturne
La main de Jacqueline X[2]
5   Que vous êtes pernicieux au fond de cette main
Yeux d'outre-temps à jamais humides
Fleur qui pourriez vous appeler la réticence du prophète
C'en est fait du présent du passé de l'avenir
Je chante la lumière unique de la coïncidence
10 La joie de m'être penché sur la grande rosace du glacier supérieur
Les infiltrations merveilleuses dont on s'aperçoit un beau jour
    qu'elles ont fait un cornet du plancher
La portée des incidents étranges mais insignifiants à première vue
Et leur don d'appropriation finale vertigineuse à moi-même
Je chante votre horizon fatal
15 Vous qui clignez imperceptiblement dans la main de mon amour
Entre le rideau de vie
Et le rideau de cœur
Yeux zinzolins
Y Z
20 De l'alphabet secret de la toute-nécessité

Zinnia-red eyes

Zinnia-red eyes[1] of the too-white little Babylonian girl
In whose navel is set a stone of the same color
When the hand of Jacqueline X[2]
Opens like a casement window onto a nocturnal garden
5   How pernicious you are in the hollow of that hand
Eyes from beyond time forever moist
Flower that could be named the prophet's reticence
The present the past the future are done with
I sing of the unique light of coincidence
10   The joy of having leaned over the great rose window in the high
      glacier
The marvelous infiltrations which are one day noticed to have made
      a cone of the wood floor
The importance of strange but at first insignificant incidents
And their power of final appropriation dizzying to me
I sing of your fatal horizon
15   You who blink imperceptibly in my love's hand
Between the life curtain
And the heart curtain
Your zinnia-red eyes
Y Z
20   Of the secret alphabet of overwhelming necessity

(JPC)

Il allait être cinq heures du matin
La barque de buée tendait sa chaîne à faire éclater les
    vitres
Et dehors
Un ver luisant
5   Soulevait comme une feuille Paris
Ce n'était qu'un cri tremblant continu
Un cri parti de l'hospice de la Maternité tout proche
FINIS FONDEUR FOU
Mais tout ce qui passait de joie dans l'exhalaison de cette douleur
10   Il me semble que j'étais tombé longtemps
J'avais encore la main crispée sur une poignée d'herbes
Et soudain ce froissement de fleurs et d'aiguilles de glace
Ces sourcils verts ce balancier d'étoile filante
De quelles profondeurs pouvait bien remonter la cloche
15   Hermétique
Dont rien la veille encore ne me faisait prévoir l'arrêt à
    ce palier
La cloche aux parois de laquelle
Ondine[1]
Tout en agitant pour t'élever la pédale du sagittaire en fer de lance[2]
20   Tu avais gravé les signes infaillibles
De mon enchantement
Au moyen d'un poignard dont le manche de corail bifurque à l'infini
Pour que ton sang et le mien
N'en fassent qu'un

It was about to be five in the morning
The skiff of steam pulled its chain so taut as to make the window-
    panes burst
And outside
A glowworm
5   Was lifting Paris like a leaf
It was but a constant quavering cry
A cry from the maternity hospital close by
FINISH FOOLISH FOUNDER
But all the joy that came through in the exhaling of that pain
10   It seems to me I'd fallen for a long time
My hand was still clasping a clump of grass
And suddenly this ruffling of flowers and ice needles
These green eyebrows this balancing-pole of a shooting star
From what depths could the bell rise
15   The hermetic bell
Whose halt at this landing nothing made me foresee the day before
The bell on whose sides
Mermaid[1]
While shaking the lanceolate archer's[2] pedal in order to rise
20   You had etched the unfailing signs
Of my enchantment
By means of a dagger whose coral handle bifurcates to infinity
So that your blood and mine
Make but one

(MAC)

Ils vont tes membres déployant autour de toi des draps verts
Et le monde extérieur
En pointillé
Ne joue plus les prairies ont déteint les jours des clochers se
    rejoignent
5   Et le puzzle social
A livré sa dernière combinaison
Ce matin encore ces draps se sont levés ont fait voile avec toi d'un lit
    prismatique
Dans le château brouillé du saule aux yeux de lama
Pour lequel la tête en bas
10   Je suis parti jadis
Draps amande de ma vie
Quand tu marches le cuivre de Vénus[1]
Innerve la feuille glissante et sans bords
Ta grande aile liquide
15   Bat dans le chant des vitriers

Your limbs go unfolding sheets of green about you
And the outer world
Speckled
Is no longer playing the meadows have faded the days of belltowers
    meet
5   And the social puzzle
Has yielded its last arrangement
This very morning again these sheets rose up set sail with you from
    a prismatic bed
In the blurred castle of the willow with llama eyes
For which upside down
10   I once set off
Sheets almond of my life
When you walk the copper of Venus[1]
Innervates the slippery edgeless leaf
Your great liquid wing
15   Flutters in the glaziers' song

(MAC)

A ta place je me méfierais du chevalier de paille
Cette espèce de Roger délivrant Angélique[1]
Leitmotiv ici des bouches de métro
Disposées en enfilade dans tes cheveux
5   C'est une charmante hallucination lilliputienne
Mais le chevalier de paille le chevalier de paille
Te prend en croupe et vous vous jetez dans la haute allée de
     peupliers
Dont les premières feuilles perdues beurrent les roses morceaux de
     pain de l'air
J'adore ces feuilles à l'égal
10 De ce qu'il y a de suprêmement indépendant en toi
Leur pâle balance
A compter de violettes
Juste ce qu'il faut pour que transparaisse aux plus tendres plis de ton
     corps
Le message indéchiffrable capital
15 D'une bouteille qui a longtemps tenu la mer
Et je les adore quand elles se rassemblent comme un coq blanc
Furieux sur le perron du château de la violence
Dans la lumière devenue déchirante où il ne s'agit plus de vivre
Dans le taillis enchanté
20 Où le chasseur épaule un fusil à crosse de faisan
Ces feuilles qui sont la monnaie de Danaë[2]
Lorsqu'il m'est donné de t'approcher à ne plus te voir
D'étreindre en toi ce lieu jaune ravagé
Le plus éclatant de ton œil
25 Où les arbres volent
Où les bâtiments commencent à être secoués d'une gaîté de mauvais
     aloi
Où les jeux du cirque se poursuivent avec un luxe effréné dans la rue
Survivre[3]
Du plus loin deux ou trois silhouettes se détachent
30 Sur le groupe étroit bat le drapeau parlementaire

If I were you I would beware of the straw knight
The Roger sort setting Angelica free[1]
Leitmotiv here of metro exits
Set all in a row in your hair
5   It's a charming Lilliputian hallucination
But the straw knight the straw knight
Takes you up behind him and you rush down the tall alley of
    poplars
Whose first lost leaves butter the roses pieces of bread from the air
I adore those leaves as much
10 As that supremely independent streak in you
Their pale balance
In accounting for violets
Just enough to make the paramount undecipherable message
Of a bottle that has long weathered the sea
15 Show through in the most tender folds of your body
And I adore them when they cluster like a white rooster
Furious on the threshold of the castle of violence
In the now rending light where it is no longer a question of
    living
In the enchanted copse
20 Where the hunter raises the pheasant-butted rifle to his shoulder
Those leaves that are the coins of Danaë[2]
When I am privileged to come so close to you that I no longer see you
To embrace in you that ravaged yellow place
The most dazzling of your eye
25 Where trees fly
Where buildings start shaking with an off-color gaiety
Where circus games go on with frenzied luxury in the street
Surviving[3]
From the furthermost point two or three silhouettes stand out
30 Over the narrow group the flag of truce is flapping

(JPC)

Toujours pour la première fois
C'est à peine si je te connais de vue
Tu rentres à telle heure de la nuit dans une maison oblique à ma
    fenêtre
Maison tout imaginaire
5   C'est là que d'une seconde à l'autre
Dans le noir intact
Je m'attends à ce que se produise une fois de plus la déchirure
    fascinante
La déchirure unique
De la façade et de mon cœur
10 Plus je m'approche de toi
En réalité
Plus la clé chante à la porte de la chambre inconnue
Où tu m'apparais seule
Tu es d'abord tout entière fondue dans le brillant
15 L'angle fugitif d'un rideau
C'est un champ de jasmin que j'ai contemplé à l'aube sur une route
    des environs de Grasse[1]
Avec ses cueilleuses en diagonale
Derrière elles l'aile sombre tombante des plants dégarnis
Devant elles l'équerre de l'éblouissant
20 Le rideau invisiblement soulevé
Rentrent en tumulte toutes les fleurs
C'est toi aux prises avec cette heure trop longue jamais assez trouble
    jusqu'au sommeil
Toi comme si tu pouvais être
La même à cela près que je ne te rencontrerai peut-être jamais
25 Tu fais semblant de ne pas savoir que je t'observe
Merveilleusement je ne suis plus sûr que tu le sais
Ton désœuvrement m'emplit les yeux de larmes
Une nuée d'interprétations entoure chacun de tes gestes
C'est une chasse à la miellée[2]

Always for the first time
I scarcely know you when I see you
You return sometime in the night to a house at an angle to
   my window
A wholly imaginary house
5   From one second to the next
There in the complete darkness
I wait for the strange rift to recur
The unique rift
In the façade and in my heart
10   The nearer I come to you
In reality
The louder the key sings in the door of the unknown
   room
Where you appear alone before me
First you merge with the brightness
15   The fleeting angle of a curtain
A jasmine field I gazed on at dawn on a road near
   Grasse[1]
The jasmine-pickers bending over on a slant
Behind them the dark profill of plants stripped bare
Before them the dazzling light
20   The curtain invisibly raised
In a frenzy all the flowers rush back in
You facing this long hour never dim enough until
   sleep
You as if you could be
The same except I may never meet you
25   You pretend not to know I'm watching you
Marvelously I am no longer sure you know it
Your idleness fills my eyes with tears
Meanings swarm around each of your gestures
Like a honeydew hunt[2]

30   Il y a des rocking-chairs sur un pont il y a des branchages qui
      risquent de t'égratigner dans la forêt
    Il y a dans une vitrine rue Notre-Dame-de-Lorette[3]
    Deux belles jambes croisées prises dans de hauts bas[4]
    Qui s'évasent au centre d'un grand trèfle blanc
    Il y a une échelle de soie déroulée sur le lierre
35   Il y a
    Qu'à me pencher sur le précipice
    De la fusion sans espoir de ta présence et de ton absence
    J'ai trouvé le secret
    De t'aimer
40   Toujours pour la première fois

30 There are rocking-chairs on a bridge there are branches that
        might scratch you in the forest
    In a window on the rue Notre-Dame-de-Lorette[3]
    Two lovely crossed legs are caught in long stockings[4]
    Flaring out in the centre of a great white clover
    There is a silken ladder unrolled across the ivy
35 There is
    That leaning over the precipice
    Of the hopeless fusion of your presence and absence
    I have found the secret
    Of loving you
40 Always for the first time

(MAC)

On me dit

On me dit que là-bas les plages sont noires
De la lave allée a la mer
Et se déroulent au pied d'un immense pic fumant de neige
Sous un second soleil de serins sauvages
5   Quel est donc ce pays lointain
Qui semble tirer toute sa lumière de ta vie
Il tremble bien réel à la pointe de tes cils
Doux à ta carnation comme un linge immatériel
Frais sorti de la malle entr'ouverte des âges
10 Derrière toi
Lançant ses derniers feux sombres entre tes jambes
Le sol du paradis perdu
Glace de ténèbres miroir d'amour
Et plus bas vers tes bras qui s'ouvrent
15 A la preuve par le printemps
D'APRÈS
De l'inexistence du mal
Tout le pommier en fleur de la mer

They tell me

They tell me that over there the beaches are black
From the lava running to the sea
Stretched out at the foot of a great peak smoking with snow
Under a second sun of wild canaries
5   So what is this far-off land
Seeming to take its light from your life
It trembles very real at the tip of your lashes
Sweet to your carnation like an intangible linen
Freshly pulled from the half-open trunk of the ages
10 Behind you
Casting its last somber fires between your legs
The earth of the lost paradise
Glass of shadows mirror of love
And lower towards your arms opening
15 On the proof by springtime
OF AFTERWARDS
Of evil's not existing
All the flowering appletree of the sea

(MAC)

From *1935–1940* in *Poèmes*
1948

Monde

Dans le salon de madame des Ricochets
Les miroirs sont en grains de rosée pressés
La console est faite d'un bras dans du lierre
Et le tapis meurt comme les vagues
5   Dans le salon de madame des Ricochets
Le thé de lune est servi dans des œufs d'engoulevent
Les rideaux amorcent la fonte des neiges
Et le piano en perspective perdue sombre d'un seul bloc dans la
    nacre
Dans le salon de madame des Ricochets
10   Des lampes basses en dessous de feuilles de tremble
Lutinent la cheminée en écailles de pangolin
Quand madame des Ricochets sonne
Les portes se fendent pour livrer passage aux servantes en
    escarpolette

World

In Madame des Ricochets' parlor
The mirrors are made of pressed beads of dew
The console is fashioned from an arm amid the ivy
And the carpet subsides like the surf
5   In Madame des Ricochets' parlor
Moon tea is served in nightjar eggs
The curtains prompt the snow to melt
And the piano in vanishing perspective sinks of a piece into
    mother-of-pearl
In Madame des Ricochets' parlor
10   Low lamps made from the underside of aspen leaves
Tease the fireplace tiled with pangolin scales
When Madame des Ricochets rings
Doors split open making way for maids swooping down in swings

(JPC)

Le Puits enchanté

Du dehors l'air est à se refroidir
Le feu éteint sous la bouillotte bleue des bois

La nature crache dans sa petite boîte de nuit[1]
Sa brosse sans épaisseur commence à faire luire les arêtes des
    buissons et des navires

5   La ville aux longues aiguillées de fulgores[2]
Monte jusqu'à se perdre
Le long d'une rampe de chansons qui tourne en vrille dans les rues
    désertes

Quand les marelles abandonnées se retournent l'une après l'autre
    dans le ciel

Tout au fond de l'entonnoir
10   Dans les fougères foulées du regard
J'ai rendez-vous avec la dame du lac

Je sais qu'elle viendra
Comme si je m'étais endormi sous des fuchsias

C'est là
15   A la place de la suspension du dessous dans la maison des nuages

Une cage d'ascenseur aux parois de laquelle éclate par touffes du
    linge de femme
De plus en plus vert

A moi

The Enchanted Well

From outside the air is fit to cool one down
The extinguished fire under the blue foot warmer in the woods

Nature spits into its small night box[1]
Its thin brush begins to make the ribs of bushes and
    ships glisten

5   The city with its long needlefuls of fulgora[2]
Rises till it vanishes
Along a ramp of songs that spirals in the deserted
    streets

When the abandoned hopscotch courts turn over one after the other
    in the sky

At the very bottom of the funnel
10   In the ferns trampled under scrutiny
I have a rendezvous with the lady of the lake

I know she will come
As if I had fallen asleep under some fuchsias

It is there
15   In the place of the suspension from underneath in the house of
    clouds

An elevator cage on whose walls women's linen bursts in tufts
Greener and greener

Come to me

A moi la fleur du grisou
20 Le ludion humain la roussette blanche[3]
La grande devinette sacrée

Mieux qu'au fil de l'eau Ophélie[4] au ballet des mouches de mai
Voici au reflet du fil à plomb celle qui est dans le secret des taupes

Je vois la semelle de poussière de diamant je vois le paon blanc qui
    fait la roue derrière l'écran de la cheminée

25 Les femmes qu'on dessine à l'envers sont les seules qu'on n'ait jamais
    vues

Son sourire est fait pour l'expiation des plongeurs de perles
Aux poumons changés en coraux

C'est Méduse casquée dont le buste pivote lentement dans la vitrine
De profil je caresse ses seins aux pointes ailées

30 Ma voix ne lui parviendrait pas ce sont deux mondes
Et même
Rien ne servirait de jeter dans sa tour une lettre toute ouverte aux
    angles de glu

On m'a passé les menottes étincelantes de Peter Ibbetson[5]

Je suis un couvreur devenu fou
35 Qui arrache par plaques et finirai bien par jeter bas tout le toit de la
    maison
Pour mieux voir comme la trombe s'élève de la mer
Pour me mêler à la bataille de fleurs
Quand une cuisse déborde l'écrin et qu'entre en jeu la pédale du
    danger

To me the fire-damp flower
20 The human bottle-imp the white pteropus[3]
The great sacred riddle

Better than Ophelia[4] aflow at the ballet of flies in May
Behold in the glint of the plumb line she who is privy to the secret
of moles

I see the sole of diamond dust I see the white peacock that spreads
its tail behind the fireplace screen

25 The women that are sketched backwards are the only ones that have
never been seen

Her smile is meant for the atonement of pearl fishers
Whose lungs turned to coral

It is Medusa in a helmet whose bust slowly swings around in the
shop window
Sideways I fondle her breasts with their winged nipples

30 My voice would not reach her they are two worlds
And even
No purpose would be served in dropping into her tower a wide open
letter with bird-lime angles

Peter Ibbetson's[5] glittering handcuffs were fastened on me

I am a crazed roofer
35 Who rips out layers at a time and soon enough shall fling down the
whole roof of the house
The better to observe how the waterspout rises from the sea
To take a part in the battle of flowers
When a thigh hangs over the jewel case and when the pedal of
danger comes into play

La belle invention
40 Pour remplacer le coucou l'horloge à escarpolette
Qui marque le temps suspendu

Pendeloque du lustre central de la terre
Mon sablier de roses
Toi qui ne remonterais pas à la surface
45 Toi qui me regardes sans me voir dans les jardins de la provocation
    pure
Toi qui m'envoies un baiser de la portière d'un train qui fuit

A beautiful invention
40 To replace the cuckoo the clock with a swing
Which registers suspended time

Pendicle from the central chandelier of the earth
My hourglass of roses
You who will not rise to the surface
45 You who look upon me without seeing me in the gardens of pure
    provocation
You who blow me a kiss from the door of a fleeing train

(JPC)

Cours-les toutes

à Benjamin Péret

Au cœur du territoire indien d'Oklahoma
Un homme assis
Dont l'œil est comme un chat qui tourne autour d'un pot de
  chiendent

Un homme cerné
5   Et par sa fenêtre
Le concile des divinités trompeuses inflexibles
Qui se lèvent chaque matin en plus grand nombre du brouillard
Fées fâchées
Vierges à l'espagnole inscrites dans un étroit triangle isocèle
10   Comètes fixes dont le vent décolore les cheveux

Le pétrole comme les cheveux d'Eléonore
Bouillonne au-dessus des continents
Et dans sa voix transparente
A perte de vue il y a des armées qui s'observent

15   Il y a des chants qui voyagent sous l'aile d'une lampe
Il y a aussi l'espoir d'aller si vite
Que dans tes yeux
Se mêlent au fil de la vitre les feuillages et les lumières

Au carrefour des routes nomades
20   Un homme
Autour de qui on a tracé un cercle
Comme autour d'une poule

Enseveli vivant dans le reflet des nappes bleues
Empilées à l'infini dans son armoire

25   Un homme à la tête cousue
Dans les bas du soleil couchant
Et dont les mains sont des poissons-coffres

Run-them-all

for Benjamin Péret

In the heart of the Indian territory of Oklahoma
A seated man
Whose eye is like a cat prowling around a pot of
    couchgrass

A surrounded man
5   And through his window
The council of deceiving inflexible deities
Who rise each morning in greater numbers from the fog
Angry fairies
Hispanesque virgins inscribed in a narrow isoceles triangle
10   Fixed comets whose hair is discolored by the wind

Petroleum like the hair of Eleanora
Seethes above the continents
And in its transparent voice
As far as the eye can see there are armies that observe each other

15   There are songs that travel under the wing of a lamp
There is also the hope of going so fast
That in your eyes
The leaves and the lights interlace across the window pane

At the crossroads of nomadic trails
20   A man
Around whom a circle is drawn
As around a hen

Buried alive in the gleam of blue sheets
Piled endlessly in his closet

25   A man with his head sewn
In the stockings of the setting sun
And whose hands are trunkfishes

Ce pays ressemble à une immense boîte de nuit
Avec ses femmes venues du bout du monde
30   Dont les épaules roulent les galets de toutes les mers
Les agences américaines n'ont pas oublié de pourvoir à ces chefs indiens
Sur les terres desquels on a foré les puits
Et qui ne restent libres de se déplacer
Que dans les limites imposées par le traité de guerre

35   La richesse inutile
Les mille paupières de l'eau qui dort

Le curateur passe chaque mois
Il pose son gibus sur le lit recouvert d'un voile de flèches
Et de sa valise de phoque
40   Se répandent les derniers catalogues des manufactures
Ailés de la main qui les ouvrait et les fermait quand nous étions
        enfants

Une fois surtout une fois
C'était un catalogue d'automobiles
Présentant la voiture de mariée
45   Au spider qui s'étend sur une dizaine de mètres
Pour la traîne
La voiture de grand peintre
Taillée dans un prisme
La voiture de gouverneur
50   Pareille à un oursin dont chaque épine est un lance-flammes

Il y avait surtout
Une voiture noire rapide
Couronnée d'aigles de nacre
Et creusée sur toutes ses facettes de rinceaux de cheminées de salon
55   Comme par les vagues
Un carrosse ne pouvant être mu que par l'éclair
Comme celui dans lequel erre les yeux fermés la princesse Acanthe[1]

This country resembles an immense night club
With its women from the ends of the earth
30 Whose shoulders make pebbles from the seven seas roll on
The American bureaus have not forgotten to provide those Indian chiefs
On whose lands wells have been drilled
And who remain free to move about
Only within the constraints set by the war treaty

35 Useless wealth
The thousand eyelids of still water

The curator comes through each month
He lays down his opera hat on a bed covered with a veil of arrows
And from his sealskin suitcase
40 Are issued the latest factory catalogs
Flown by the hand that spread and shut them when we were
   children

Once especially once
It was an automobile catalog
Showing a bride's car
45 To the rumble seat stretching over ten or so meters
For the dress train
The great painter's car
Hewn in a prism
The governor's car
50 Similar to a sea urchin each of whose spines is a flame thrower

There was especially
A fast black car
Crowned with mother-of-pearl eagles
And carved on all its facets with the foliated molding of living room
   fireplaces
55 As by waves
A coach movable only by a flash
Such as the one in which Princess Acantha[1] wanders with her eyes
   closed

Une brouette géante toute en limaces grises
Et en langues de feu comme celle qui apparaît aux heures fatales
    dans le jardin de la tour Saint-Jacques[2]
60   Un poisson rapide pris dans une algue et multipliant les coups de
    queue

Une grande voiture d'apparat et de deuil
Pour la dernière promenade d'un saint empereur à venir
De fantaisie
Qui démoderait la vie entière

65   Le doigt a désigné sans hésitation l'image glacée
Et depuis lors
L'homme à la crête de triton
A son volant de perles
Chaque soir vient border le lit de la déesse du maïs

70   Je garde pour l'histoire poétique
Le nom de ce chef dépossédé qui est un peu le nôtre
De cet homme seul engagé dans le grand circuit
De cet homme superbement rouillé dans une machine neuve
Qui met le vent en berne

75   Il s'appelle
Il porte le nom flamboyant de Cours-les toutes
A la vie à la mort cours à la fois les deux lièvres
Cours ta chance qui est une volée de cloches de fête et d'alarme
Cours les créatures de tes rêves qui défaillent rouées à leurs jupons
    blancs
80   Cours la bague sans doigt
Cours la tête de l'avalanche

29 octobre 1938

A giant wheelbarrow all made up of grey slugs
And of tongues of fire such as the one that appears at fateful times
    in the gardens of the Tour Saint-Jacques[2]
60 A nimble fish caught in seaweed and repeatedly flicking its tail

A big ceremonial and funeral car
For the last ride of a future holy emperor
Fanciful
That would cause one's whole life to go out of fashion

65 The finger has unhesitatingly pointed out the icy image
And since then
The man with a triton crest
At his pearly steering wheel
Each evening comes and tucks in the corn goddess' bed

70 I keep for poetical history
The name of that dispossessed chief who is somewhat our own
Of that single man advancing down the full circuit
Of that superbly rusted man in a new machine
That puts the wind at half mast

75 He is called
He bears the flamboyant name of Run-them-all
In life in death run down all your leads at once
Run up your luck which is a full peal of bells in celebration and
    alarm
Run for the creatures of your dreams who faint away lashed to their
    white petticoats
80 Run the fingerless ring
Run the tip of the avalanche

October 29, 1938

(JPC)

Quels apprêts

Les armoires bombées de la campagne
Glissent silencieusement sur les rails de lait
C'est l'heure où les filles soulevées par le flot de la nuit qui roule des
    carlines
Se raidissent contre la morsure de l'hermine
5   Dont le cri
Va mouler les pointes de leur gorge

        Les événements d'un autre ordre sont absolument
            dépourvus d'intérêt
        Ne me parlez pas de ce papier mural à décor de ronces
        Qui n'a rien de plus pressé
10   Que de se lacérer lui-même

Les flammes noires luttent dans la grille avec des langues d'herbe
Un galop lointain
C'est la charge souterraine sonnée dans le bois de violette et dans le
    buis
Toute la chambre se renverse
15 Le splendide alignement des mesures d'étain s'épuise en une seule
        qui par surcroît est le vin gris
La cuisse toujours trop tôt dépêchée sur le tableau de craie dans la
    tourmente de jour

        Les gisements d'hommes les lacs de murmures
        La pensée tirant sur son collier de vieilles niches
        Qu'on me laisse une fois pour toutes avec cela

20 Les diables-mouches voient dans ces ongles
    Les pépins du quartier de pomme de la rosée
    Ramené du fond de la vie

What Frills

The bulging cabinets of the countryside
Silently glide upon rails of milk
It's that time when girls raised by the tide of night that carries
    thistles
Brace themselves against the ermine's bite
5   Whose cry
Will outline their bosom tips

    Events of another order are absolutely devoid of
        interest
    Don't mention that bramble-patterned wallpaper
    That has nothing more urgent
10   Than to lacerate itself

Black flames wrestle in the grate with tongues of grass
A faraway gallop
It's the subterranean charge sounded in the grove of violet and in
    boxwood
The whole room turns upside down
15   The splendid alignment of tin gauges dwindles down to a single one
    which is grey wine to boot
The all too hasty thigh on the chalkboard in the daystorm

    Lodes of men lakes of whispers
    Thought pulling on its collar of old doghouses
    May I be left with that once and for all

20   The devil-flies see in these fingernails
Pips of the apple wedge of the dew
Brought forth from the depths of life

Le corps tout en poissons surgit du filet ruisselant
Dans la brousse
25   De l'air autour du lit
L'argus de la dérive chère les yeux fixes mi-ouverts mi-clos

Poitiers, 9 mai 1940

The body all made of fishes emerges from the dripping net
In the bush
25   Air around the bed
The argus of dear drift eyes staring half open half shut

Poitiers, May 9, 1940

(JPC)

Fata Morgana
1940

Fata Morgana[I]

Ce matin la fille de la montagne tient sur ses genoux un accordéon
    de chauves-souris blanches
Un jour un nouveau jour cela me fait penser à un objet que je garde
Alignés en transparence dans un cadre des tubes en verre de toutes
    les couleurs de philtres de liqueurs
Qu'avant de me séduire il ait dû répondre peu importe à quelque
    nécessité de représentation commerciale
5   Pour moi nulle œuvre d'art ne vaut ce petit carré fait de l'herbe
    diaprée à perte de vue de la vie
Un jour un nouvel amour et je plains ceux pour qui l'amour perd à
    ne pas changer de visage
Comme si de l'étang sans lumière la carpe qui me tend à l'éveil une
    boucle de tes cheveux
N'avait plus de cent ans et ne me taisait tout ce que je dois pour
    rester moi-même ignorer
Un nouveau jour est-ce bien près de toi que j'ai dormi
10   J'ai donc dormi j'ai donc passé les gants de mousse
Dans l'angle je commence à voir briller la mauvaise commode qui
    s'appelle hier
Il y a de ces meubles embarrassants dont le véritable office est de
    cacher des issues
De l'autre côté qui sait la barque aimantée nous pourrions partir
    ensemble
A la rencontre de l'arbre sous l'écorce duquel il est dit
15   Ce qu'à nous seuls nous sommes l'un à l'autre dans la grande algèbre
Il y a de ces meubles plus lourds que s'ils étaient emplis de sable au
    fond de la mer
Contre eux il faudrait des mots-leviers
De ces mots échappés d'anciennes chansons qui vont au superbe
    paysage de grues[2]
Très tard dans les ports parcourus en zigzag de bouquets de fièvre
20   Ecoute
Je vois le lutin
Que d'un ongle tu mets en liberté

Fata Morgana[I]

This morning the mountain's daughter is holding on her lap an
accordion of white bats
One day a new day it makes me think of an object I am keeping
Transparently aligned in a frame glass tubes in all colors of philtres
of liqueurs
That before enticing me it must have served it doesn't matter some
purpose as a commercial sample
5   For me no work of art is worth that little square made of variegated
grass as far as the eye of life can see
One day a new love and I pity those for whom love loses if it keeps
the same face
As if from the lightless pool the carp holding out a lock of your hair
as I awaken
Weren't over a hundred and didn't keep from me all I should not
know in order to remain true to myself
A new day is it really near you that I slept
10   So I slept so I put on moss gloves
In the corner I am beginning to see the mean chest of drawers called
yesterday gleaming
The real function of some of those awkward pieces of furniture is to
hide the exits
On the other side who knows the magnetic ship we might be able to
sail away together
In quest of the tree under whose bark it is said
15   What we alone are to each other in the great algebra
Some furniture is heavier than if it were filled with sand at the
bottom of the sea
Against it you'd have to use lever-words
Words broken loose from old songs heading for the superb land-
scape of cranes[2]
Very late in ports criss-crossed by fever bouquets
20   Listen
I see the sprite
That you are releasing with a fingernail

En ouvrant un paquet de cigarettes
Le héraut-mouche qui jette le sel de la mode
25   Si zélé à faire croire que tout ne doit pas être de toujours
Celui qui exulte à faire dire Allo je n'entends plus

Comme c'est joli qu'est-ce que ça rappelle

Si j'étais une ville dis-tu Tu serais Ninive sur le Tigre
Si j'étais un instrument de travail Plût au ciel noir tu serais la canne
    des cueilleurs dans les verreries
30   Si j'étais un symbole Tu serais une fougère dans une nasse
Et si j'avais un fardeau à porter Ce serait une boule faite de têtes
    d'hermines qui crient
Si je devais fuir la nuit sur une route Ce serait le sillage du
    géranium
Si je pouvais voir derrière moi sans me retourner Ce serait
    l'orgueil de la torpille

Comme c'est joli

35   En un rien de temps
Il faut convenir qu'on a vu s'évanouir dans un rêve
Les somptueuses robes en tulle pailleté des arroseuses municipales
Et même plier bagage sous le regard glacial de l'amiral Coligny[3]
Le dernier vendeur de papier d'Arménie[4]
40   De nos jours songe qu'une expédition se forme pour la capture de
    l'oiseau quetzal dont on ne possède plus en vie oui en vie que
    quatre exemplaires
Qu'on a vu tourner à blanc la roulette des marchands de plaisir

Qu'est-ce que ça rappelle

Dans les hôtels à plantes vertes c'est l'heure où les charnières des
    portes sans nombre
D'un coup d'archet s'apprêtent à séparer comme les oiseaux les
    chaussures les mieux accordées

When you open a cigarette pack
The herald-fly flinging the salt of fashion
25   So eagerly bent upon making you believe that everything doesn't
      have to be timeless
The one who rejoices in making you say Hello I can't hear you now

How lovely what does that bring to mind

If I were a town you are saying You would be Nineveh on the Tigris
If I were a work tool For black heaven's sake you would be the
      pickers' cane in the glassworks
30   If I were a symbol You would be a fern in a lobster trap
And if I had a bundle to carry It would be a ball of wailing
      ermine-heads
If I had to flee at night on a road It would be the geranium's furrow
If I could see behind me without looking back It would be the pride
      of the torpedo fish

How lovely

35   In no time at all
You have to admit we have seen these vanish in a dream
The sumptuous dresses of spangled tulle worn by the women
      tending the city watering-carts
And even pack up under the icy stare of Admiral Coligny[3]
The last scented-candle seller[4]
40   In our time just think an expedition is forming to capture the quetzal
      bird of which only four are held alive yes alive
We have seen the roulette wheel of the pleasure vendors turning white

What does that bring to mind

In the hotels full of green plants this is the time when the hinges of
      numberless doors
With one stroke of the bow are ready to separate like birds the
      best-tuned shoes

45   Sur les paliers mordorés[5] dans le moule à gaufre fracassé où se
      cristallise le bismuth
      A la lumière des châteaux vitrifiés du mont Knock-Farril dans le
      comté de Ross[6]
      Un jour un nouveau jour cela me fait penser à un objet que garde
      mon ami Wolfgang Paalen[7]
      D'une corde déjà grise tous les modèles de nœuds réunis sur une
      planchette
      Je ne sais pourquoi il déborde tant le souci didactique qui a présidé à
      sa construction sans doute pour une école de marins
50   Bien que l'ingéniosité de l'homme donne ici sa fleur que nimbe la
      nuée des petits singes aux yeux pensifs
      En vérité aucune page des livres même virant au pain bis n'atteint à
      cette vertu conjuratoire rien ne m'est si propice
      Un nouvel amour et que d'autres tant pis se bornent à adorer
      La bête aux écailles de roses aux flancs creux dont j'ai trompé depuis
      longtemps la vigilance
      Je commence à voir autour de moi dans la grotte
55   Le vent lucide m'apporte le parfum perdu de l'existence
      Quitte enfin de ses limites
      A cette profondeur je n'entends plus sonner que le patin
      Dont parfois l'éclair livre toute une perspective d'armoires à glace[8]
      écroulées avec leur linge
      Parce que tu tiens
60   Dans mon être la place du diamant serti dans une vitre
      Qui me détaillerait avec minutie le gréement des astres[9]
      Deux mains qui se cherchent c'est assez pour le toit de demain
      Deux mains transparentes la tienne le murex dont les anciens ont
      tiré mon sang
      Mais voici que la nappe ailée
65   S'approche encore léchée de la flamme des grands vins
      Elle comble les arceaux d'air boit d'un trait les lacunes des feuilles
      Et joue à se faire prendre en écharpe par l'aqueduc
      Qui roule des pensées sauvages

45   On the bronze landings[5] in the shattered waffle iron where bismuth
      turns to crystal
     In the light of the vitrified castles of Mount Knock-Farril in County
      Ross[6]
     One day a new day that makes me think of an object kept by my
      friend Wolfgang Paalen[7]
     From a rope already grey all the kinds of knots assembled on a plank
     I don't know why it goes beyond far beyond the didactic concern
      that guided its construction doubtless for a seafarers' school
50   Although human cleverness here brings forth its full flower edged
      with a bright cloud of tiny monkeys with thoughtful eyes
     Really not one page of the books even turning to brown bread
      reaches this exorcising power nothing is so propitious to me
     A new love and too bad may others confine themselves to adoring
     The hollow-flanked beast with rose scales whose vigilance I have
      eluded for a long time
     I begin to see around me in the grotto
55   The lucid wind brings me the lost perfume of existence
     Finally free of its limits
     At such a depth I hear nothing but the skate resounding
     Whose flash sometimes yields a whole perspective of mirror-ward-
      robes[8] collapsed with their clothing
     Because you hold
60   Within me the place of the diamond set in a pane of glass
     That would point out to me in minute detail the rigging of the
      stars[9]
     Two hands seeking each other suffice for tomorrow's roof
     Two transparent hands yours the murex from which the ancients
      drew my blood
     But now the winged tablecloth
65   Comes nearer still licked by the flame of great wines
     It fills the arches of air drinks in one gulp the air cells in the leaves
     And plays at being sideswiped by the aqueduct
     Driven by wild thoughts

Les bulles qui montent à la surface du café
70   Après le sucre le charmant usage populaire qui veut que les prélève
la cuiller
Ce sont autant de baisers égarés
Avant qu'elles ne courent s'anéantir contre les bords
O tourbillon plus savant que la rose
Tourbillon qui emporte l'esprit qui me regagne à l'illusion enfantine
75   Que tout est là pour quelque chose qui me concerne

Qu'est-ce qui est écrit
Il y a ce qui est écrit sur nous et ce que nous écrivons
Où est la grille qui montrerait que si son tracé extérieur
Cesse d'être juxtaposable à son tracé intérieur
80   La main passe

Plus à portée de l'homme il est d'autres coïncidences
Véritables fanaux dans la nuit du sens
C'était plus qu'improbable c'est donc *exprès*
Mais les gens sont si bien en train de se noyer
85   Que ne leur demandez pas[10] de saisir la perche

Le lit fonce sur ses rails de miel bleu
Libérant en transparence les animaux de la sculpture médiévale
Il incline prêt à verser au ras des talus de digitales
Et s'éclaire par intermittence d'yeux d'oiseaux de proie
90   Chargés de tout ce qui émane du gigantesque casque emplumé
d'Otrante[11]
Le lit fonce sur ses rails de miel bleu
Il lutte de vitesse avec les ciels changeants
Qui conviennent toujours ascension des piques de clôture des parcs
Et boucanage de plus belle succédant au lever de danseuses sur le
comptoir
95   Le lit brûle les signaux il ne fait qu'un de tous les bocaux de poissons
rouges
Il lutte de vitesse avec les ciels changeants
Rien de commun tu sais avec le petit chemin de fer

The bubbles rising to the surface of the coffee
70 After the sugar the charming popular custom according to which the
    spoon gathers them up
Like so many stray kisses
Before they rush to oblivion against the rim
O whirlwind wiser than the rose
Whirlwind that sweeps away the mind that wins me back to the
    childlike illusion
75 That all is there for something that affects me

What is written
There is what is written on us and what we write
Where is the grid showing that if its exterior outline
No longer fits alongside its interior outline
80 The hand passes

More within human reach there are other coincidences
Real beacons in the night of meaning
It was more than improbable it must then be *on purpose*
But people are so well on the way to drowning themselves
85 That don't ask them[10] to grab the pole being held out for them

The bed hurtles along on its rails of blue honey
Freeing into transparency the animals of medieval sculpture
It tilts ready to turn over on its side flush with the slopes of foxglove
And is lit intermittently by the eyes of birds of prey
90 Filled with all the emanations of the gigantic plumed helmet of
    Otranto[11]
The bed hurtles along on its rails of blue honey
It tries to outpace the changing skies
That always concur ascension of park-fence spikes
And more smoking than ever following the dancers as they rise up
    on the counter
95 The bed runs the red lights runs all the goldfish bowls together
It tries to outpace the changing skies
Nothing in common you know with the little railroad

Qui se love à Cordoba du Mexique pour que nous ne nous lassions
    pas de découvrir
Les gardénias qui embaument dans de jeunes pousses de palmier
    évidées
100   Ou ailleurs pour nous permettre de choisir
Du marchepied dans les lots d'opales et de turquoises brutes
Non le lit à folles aiguillées[12] ne se borne pas à dérouler la soie des
    lieux et des jours incomparables
Il est le métier sur lequel se croisent les cycles et d'où sourd ce qu'on
    pressent sous le nom de musique des sphères
Le lit brûle les signaux il ne fait qu'un de tous les bocaux de poissons
    rouges
105   Et quand il va pour fouiller en sifflant le tunnel charnel
Les murs s'écartent la vieille poudre d'or à n'y plus voir se lève des
    registres d'état-civil
Enfin tout est repris par le mouvement de la mer
Non le lit à folles aiguillées ne se borne pas à dérouler la soie des
    lieux et des jours incomparables

C'est la pièce sans entractes le rideau levé une fois pour toutes sur la
    cascade
110   Dis-moi
Comment se défendre en voyage de l'arrière-pensée pernicieuse
Que l'on ne se rend pas où l'on voudrait
La petite place qui fuit entourée d'arbres qui diffèrent
    imperceptiblement de tous les autres
Existe pour que nous la traversions sous tel angle dans la vraie vie
115   Le ruisseau en cette boucle même comme en nulle autre de tous les
    ruisseaux
Est maître d'un secret qu'il ne peut faire nôtre à la volée
Derrière la fenêtre celle-ci faiblement lumineuse entre bien d'autres
    plus ou moins lumineuses
Ce qui *se passe*
Est de toute importance pour nous peut-être faudrait-il revenir
120   Avoir le courage de sonner
Qui dit qu'on ne nous accueillerait pas à bras ouverts

Coiling in Cordoba Mexico so that we never tire of
    discovering
Gardenias in full scent in the young hollowed-out
    palm shoots
100 Or elsewhere to enable us to choose
From the footboard among the batches of opals and rough
    turquoise
No the bed with its crazy threadlengths[12] does not confine itself to
    unrolling the silk of incomparable places and days
It is the loom on which cycles cross and from which wells up the
    foreboding of what is known as the music of the spheres
The bed runs the red lights runs all the goldfish bowls together
105 And when it delves whistling into the carnal tunnel
The walls spread apart the old gold dust so thick as to obscure one's
    vision rises from the official registers
Finally everything is caught up in the movement of the sea
No the bed with its crazy threadlengths does not confine itself to
    unrolling the silk of incomparable places and days

It's the play without intermission the curtain raised once and forever
    on the waterfall
110 Tell me
How to prevent yourself while traveling from having in the back of
    your mind the pernicious thought
That you are not going where you would like to
The little square fleeing surrounded by trees imperceptibly different
    from all the others
Exists for us to cross it at such and such an angle in real life
115 The stream in this very curve as in no other of all the streams
Is the master of a secret it cannot make ours in a rush
Behind the window this one faintly luminous among many others
    more or less luminous
What *is happening*
Is of prime importance for us perhaps we should go back
120 Pluck up our courage and ring
Who is to say we wouldn't be welcomed with open arms

Mais rien n'est vérifié tous ont peur nous-mêmes
Avons presque aussi peur
Et pourtant je suis sûr qu'au fond du bois fermé à clé qui tourne en
ce moment contre la vitre
125 S'ouvre la seule clairière
Est-ce là l'amour cette promesse qui nous dépasse
Ce billet d'aller et retour éternel établi sur le modèle de la phalène
chinée
Est-ce l'amour ces doigts qui pressent la cosse du brouillard
Pour qu'en jaillissent les villes inconnues aux portes hélas
éblouissantes
130 L'amour ces fils télégraphiques qui font de la lumière insatiable un
brillant sans cesse qui se rouvre
De la taille[13] même de notre compartiment de la nuit
Tu viens à moi de plus loin que l'ombre je ne dis pas dans l'espace
des séquoias millénaires
Dans ta voix se font la courte échelle des trilles d'oiseaux perdus
Beaux dés pipés[14]
135 Bonheur et malheur
Au bonneteau tous ces yeux écarquillés autour d'un
parapluie ouvert
Quelle revanche le santon-puce de la bohémienne
Ma main se referme sur elle
Si j'échappais à mon destin

140 Il faut chasser le vieil aveugle des lichens du mur d'église
Détruire jusqu'au dernier les horribles petits folios déteints jaunes
verts bleus roses
Ornés d'une fleur variable et exsangue
Qu'il vous invite à détacher de sa poitrine
Un à un contre quelques sous

145 Mais toujours force reste
Au langage ancien les simples la marmite
Une chevelure qui vient au feu

But nothing is verified everyone is afraid we ourselves
Are almost as afraid
And yet I am sure that deep in the wood under lock and key turning
    at this moment against the glass pane
125 There opens the single clearing
Is it love that promise which is beyond us
That eternal round-trip ticket written on the model of the mottled
    moth
Is it love those fingers pressing the husk of mist
So that unknown towns burst forth from them with alas dazzling
    doors
130 Love those telegraph wires which from the insatiable light make a
    diamond reopening ceaselessly
Cut to the size[13] of our compartment of night
You come to me from beyond the shadows I am not saying in the
    space of thousand-year-old sequoias
In your voice trills of lost birds give themselves a lift
Lovely loaded dice[14]
135 Fortune and misfortune
In the three-card trick all those wide-eyed stares around an open
    umbrella
What revenge the flea-figurine of the bohemian
My hand closes on her
If I were to escape from my fate

140 You have to send away the old blind man from the lichens of the
    church wall
Destroy to the very last those horrid little folios faded yellow green
    blue pink
Trimmed with a variable and bloodless flower
That he invites you to take off his chest
One by one for a few pennies

145 But strength ever remains
In the old language the simple ones the cooking pot
A mane of hair coming to the fire

Et quoi qu'on fasse jamais happé au cœur de toute lumière
Le drapeau des pirates

150   *Un homme grand engagé sur un chemin périlleux[15]*
    Il ne s'est pas contenté de passer sous un bleu d'ouvrier les brassards à
        pointes acérées d'un criminel célèbre
    A sa droite le lion dans sa main l'oursin
    Se dirige vers l'est
    Où déjà le tétras gonfle de vapeur et de bruit sourd les airelles
155   *Voilà qu'il tente de franchir le torrent les pierres qui sont des lueurs*
        d'épaules de femmes au théâtre
    Pivotent en vain très lentement
    J'avais cessé de le voir il reparaît un peu plus bas sur l'autre berge
    Il s'assure qu'il est toujours porteur de l'oursin
    A sa droite le lion all right[16]
160   *Le sol qu'il effleure à peine crépite de débris de faulx*
    En même temps cet homme descend précipitamment un escalier au cœur
        d'une ville il a déposé sa cuirasse
    Au dehors on se bat contre ce qui ne peut plus durer
    Cet homme parmi tant d'autres brusquement semblables
    Qu'est-il donc que se sent-il donc de plus que lui-même
165   *Pour que ce qui ne peut plus*
                    durer ne dure plus
    Il est tout prêt à ne plus durer lui-même
    Un pour tous advienne que pourra
    Ou la vie serait la goutte de poison
170   *Du non-sens introduite dans le chant de l'alouette au-dessus des coquelicots*
    La rafale passe

    En même temps
    Cet homme qui relevait des casiers autour du phare
    Hésite à rentrer il soulève avec précaution des algues et des algues
175   *Le vent est tombé ainsi soit-il*
    Et encore des algues qu'il repose
    Comme s'il lui était interdit de découvrir dans son ensemble le jeune corps
        de femme le plus secret

And whatever is done never snatched at the heart of any light
The pirates' flag

150 *A tall man treading a perilous path[15]*
It wasn't enough for him to slip on the sharp pointed armbands of some
famous criminal under his blue overalls
At his right the lion in his hand the sea-urchin
Is eastward bound
Where already the grouse puffs up the whortleberry with steam and
muffled sound
155 *There he is trying to cross the torrent the stones gleaming shoulders of*
women at the theater
Vainly swivel very slowly
I had stopped seeing him he reappears a little lower on the other bank
He makes sure he is still bearing the sea-urchin
At his right the lion ça va[16]
160 *The ground he barely skims over crackles with the scythes' debris*
Meanwhile this man quickly goes down a stair in the heart of a town he
has laid down his breastplate
Outside a battle is being waged against what can last no longer
This man among so many others suddenly similar
What is he then what does he feel then more than himself
165 *So that what can no longer last*
                    will last no longer
He is quite ready not to last longer himself
One for all come what may
Or life would be the drop of poison
170 *Of nonsense introduced in the song of the lark above the poppies*
The gust of wind passes

Meanwhile
The man who took up lobster traps around the lighthouse
Hesitates to go back in he cautiously lifts up algae and more algae
175 *The wind has fallen so be it*
And again algae which he puts down
As if he were forbidden to discover in its totality a young woman's body at
its most secret

D'où part une construction ailée
Ici le temps se brouille à la fois et s'éclaire
180   *Du trapèze tout en cigale[17]*
Mystérieusement une très petite fille interroge
André tu ne sais pas pourquoi je résédise[18]
Et aussitôt une pyramide s'élance au loin
A la vie à la mort ce qui commence me précède et m'achève
185   *Une fine pyramide à jour de pierre dure*
Reliée à ce beau corps par des lacets vermeils

De la brune à la blonde
Entre le chaume et la couche de terreau
Il y a place pour mille et une cloches de verre
190   Sous lesquelles revivent sans fin les têtes qui m'enchantent
Dans la suspension du sacre
Têtes de femmes qui se succèdent sur tes épaules quand tu dors
Il en est de si lointaines
Têtes d'hommes aussi
195   Innombrables à commencer par ces chefs d'empereurs à la barbe
        glissante
Le maraîcher va et vient sous sa housse
Il embrasse d'un coup d'œil tous les plateaux montés cette nuit du
        centre de la terre
Un nouveau jour c'est lui et tous ces êtres
Aisément reconnaissables dans les vapeurs de la campagne
200   C'est toi c'est moi à tâtons sous l'éternel déguisement

Dans les entrelacs de l'histoire momie d'ibis
Un pas pour rien comme on cargue la voilure momie d'ibis
Ce qui sort du côté cour rentre par le côté jardin momie d'ibis
Si le développement de l'enfant permet qu'il se libère du fantasme de
        démembrement de dislocation du corps momie d'ibis
205   Il ne sera jamais trop tard pour en finir avec le morcelage de l'âme
        momie d'ibis
Et par toi seule sous toutes ses facettes de momie d'ibis

From which a winged construction extends
Here the weather is clouding over and clearing up at once
180 *From the trapeze completely in squillfishes¹⁷*
Mysteriously a tiny little girl questions
André you don't know why I mignonette¹⁸
And at once a pyramid rushes into the distance
For life for death what begins precedes me and finishes me
185 *A slender pyramid in hardstone daylight*
Linked to this lovely body by crimson laces

From the brunette to the blonde
Between the thatch and the compost layer
There is room for a thousand and one glass bells
190 Under which the heads that delight me live endlessly once more
In the suspension of solemn rites
Heads of women following one another on your shoulders when you
    sleep
There are such distant ones
Heads of men also
195 Countless beginning with those emperor heads with slippery beards
The market gardener comes and goes under his horsecloth
He sees at a glance all the plateaus risen last night from the center
    of the earth
A new day he and all those beings
Easily recognized in the mists of the countryside
200 You me groping under the eternal disguise

In the skeins of history ibis mummy
A step for nothing as the sails are taken in ibis mummy
What goes out stage left comes back in stage right ibis mummy
If the child's development lets him shake off the fantasm of
    dismembering of bodily dislocation ibis mummy
205 It will never be too late to have done with the parceling up of
    the soul ibis mummy
And by you alone under all its facets of ibis mummy

Avec tout ce qui n'est plus ou attend d'être je retrouve l'unité perdue
momie d'ibis
Momie d'ibis du non-choix à travers ce qui me parvient
Momie d'ibis qui veut que tout ce que je puis savoir contribue à moi
sans distinction
210   Momie d'ibis qui me fait l'égal tributaire du mal et du bien
Momie d'ibis du sort goutte à goutte où l'homéopathie dit son grand
mot
Momie d'ibis de la quantité se muant dans l'ombre en qualité
Momie d'ibis de la combustion qui laisse en toute cendre un point
rouge
Momie d'ibis de la perfection qui appelle la fusion incessante des
créatures imparfaites
215   La gangue des statues ne me dérobe de moi-même que ce qui n'est
pas le produit aussi précieux de la semence des gibets momie d'ibis
Je suis Nietzsche commençant à comprendre qu'il est à la fois
Victor-Emmanuel et deux assassins des journaux Astu[19] momie
d'ibis
C'est à moi seul que je dois tout ce qui s'est écrit pensé chanté
momie d'ibis
Et sans partage toutes les femmes de ce monde je les ai aimées
momie d'ibis
Je les ai aimées pour t'aimer mon unique amour momie d'ibis
220   Dans le vent du calendrier dont les feuilles s'envolent momie d'ibis
En vue de ce reposoir dans le bois momie d'ibis sur le parcours du
lactaire délicieux

Ouf le basilic est passé tout près sans me voir
Qu'il revienne je tiens braqué sur lui le miroir
Où est faite pour se consommer la jouissance humaine
imprescriptible
225   Dans une convulsion que termine un éclaboussement de plumes
dorées
Il faudrait marquer ici de sanglots non seulement les attitudes du
buste
Mais encore les effacements et les oppositions de la tête

With all that is no more or is waiting to be I rediscover unity lost
   ibis mummy
Ibis mummy of choicelessness across what reaches me
Ibis mummy requiring that all I might know contribute to me with-
   out distinction
210   Ibis mummy making me the tributary of evil and good alike
Ibis mummy of chance drop by drop where homeopathy has its big
   word to say
Ibis mummy of quantity molting into quality in the shadows
Ibis mummy of combustion leaving in every cinder a
   red dot
Ibis mummy of perfection summoning the incessant fusion of
   imperfect creatures
215   The matrix of statues takes away from me only what is not the so
   precious product of the seed of gallows ibis mummy
I am Nietzsche beginning to understand that he is at once Victor-
   Emmanuel and two assassins in the newspapers Astu[19] ibis
   mummy
It is to myself alone that I owe everything that is written thought
   sung ibis mummy
And without sharing them I've loved all the women of this world
   ibis mummy
I have loved them so as to love you my unique love ibis mummy
220   In the wind of the calendar whose leaves are flying off ibis mummy
In sight of that resting-place in the wood ibis mummy on the path
   of the saffron milk cap

Whew the basilisk passed close by without seeing me
Just let him come back I've got my mirror trained on him
Unprescribable human joy is made there to be
   consummated
225   In a convulsion ended by a splash of gilded feathers
It would be appropriate to mark with sobs here not only the
   positions of the bust
But also the blurrings and the oppositions of the head

Le problème reste plus ou moins posé en chorégraphie
Où non plus je ne sache pas qu'on ait trouvé de mesure pour l'éperdu
230 Quand la coupe ce sont précisément les lèvres
Dans cette accélération où défilent
Sous réserve de contrôle
Au moment où l'on se noie les menus faits de la vie
Mais les cabinets d'antiques abondent en pierres d'Abraxas[20]
235 Trois cent soixante-cinq fois plus méchantes que le jour solaire
Et l'œuf religieux du coq
Continue à être couvé religieusement par le crapaud

Du vieux balcon qui ne tient plus que par un fil de lierre
Il arrive que le regard errant sur les dormantes eaux du fossé
        circulaire
240 Surprenne en train de se jouer le progrès hermétique
Tout de feinte et dont on ne saurait assez redouter
La séduction infinie
A l'en croire rien ne manque qui ne soit donné en puissance et c'est
        vrai ou presque
La belle lumière électrique pourvu que cela ne te la fane pas de
        penser qu'un jour elle paraîtra jaune
245 De haute lutte la souffrance a bien été chassée de quelques-uns de
        ses fiefs
Et les distances peuvent continuer à fondre
Certains vont même jusqu'à soutenir qu'il n'est pas impossible que
        l'homme
Cesse de dévorer l'homme bien qu'on n'avance guère de ce côté
Cependant cette suite de prestiges je prendrai garde comme une toile
        d'araignée étincelante
250 Qu'elle ne s'accroche à mon chapeau
Tout ce qui vient à souhait est à double face et fallacieux
Le meilleur à nouveau s'équilibre de pire
Sous le bandeau de fusées
Il n'est que de fermer les yeux
255 Pour retrouver la table du permanent

The problem remains more or less posed in choreography
Where I don't know either if any measure has been found for the
    madcap
230 When the lips are precisely that cup
In this acceleration where life's petty events flash by
Subject to control
At the moment of drowning
But the collections of antiques abound in Abraxas stones[20]
235 Three hundred and sixty-five times nastier than the solar day
And the religious egg of the rooster
Continues to be brooded religiously by the toad

From the old balcony which barely hangs by a single tendril of ivy
It happens that the look wandering over the sleeping waters of the
    circular moat
240 Surprises hermetic progress in the act of play
In all its feints and whose infinite attractiveness
Is to be ever dreaded
To take its word for it nothing is lacking which is not potentially
    granted and that is true or almost
The lovely electric light so long as thinking that it will seem yellow
    one day does not make it wither for you
245 After a noble struggle suffering has indeed been driven out of some
    of its fiefdoms
And distances can continue to melt away
Some go so far as to maintain that it isn't impossible that man
Might stop devouring man although hardly any progress is being
    made in this respect
Nevertheless I will take care that this series of marvels like a
    sparkling spider web
250 Doesn't catch on my hat
Everything that occurs as one wishes is double-faced and deceptive
Again the best is counterbalanced by the worst
Under the blindfold of rockets
You need only close your eyes
255 To find the table of the permanent again

Ceci dit la représentation continue
Eu égard ou non à l'actualité
L'action se passe dans le voile du hennin d'Isabeau de Bavière[21]
Toutes dentelles et moires
260   Aussi fluides que l'eau qui fait la roue au soleil sur les glaces des
       fleuristes d'aujourd'hui
Le cerf blanc à reflets d'or sort du bois du Châtelet
Premier plan[22] de ses yeux qui expriment le rêve des chants d'oiseaux
       du soir
Dans l'obliquité du dernier rayon le sens d'une révélation
       mystérieuse
Que sais-je encore et qu'on sait capables de pleurer
265   Le cerf ailé frémit il fond sur l'aigle avec l'épée[23]
Mais l'aigle est partout
                              sus à lui
                                        il y a eu l'avertissement
De cet homme dont les chroniqueurs s'obstinent à rapporter dans
       une intention qui leur échappe
270   Qu'il était vêtu de blanc de cet homme bien entendu qu'on ne
       retrouvera pas
Puis la chute d'une lance contre un casque ici le musicien a fait
       merveille
C'est toute la raison qui s'en va[24] quand l'heure pourrait être frappée
       sans que tu y sois

Dans les ombres du décor le peuple est admis à contempler les
       grands festins
On aime toujours beaucoup voir manger sur la scène
275   De l'intérieur du pâté couronné de faisans
Des nains d'un côté noirs de l'autre arc-en-ciel soulèvent le
       couvercle
Pour se répandre dans un harnachement de grelots et de rires
Eclat *contrasté* de traces de coups de feu de la croûte qui tourne
Enchaîné sur le bal des Ardents[25] *rappel en trouble* de l'épisode qui
       suit de près celui du cerf

That being understood the performance goes on
Irrespective of current events or not
The action happens in the veil of Isabel of Bavaria's headpiece[21]
All lace and moiré silk
260   As fluid as water turning cartwheels in the sun on the mirrors of
today's florists
The white stag with golden flecks emerges from the Châtelet woods
Close-up[22] of his eyes expressing the dream of the songs of evening
birds
In the oblique angle of the last beam the meaning of a mysterious
revelation
Goodness knows what else and whose eyes we know are capable of
weeping
265   The winged stag shivers he pounces on the eagle with the sword[23]
But the eagle is everywhere
get him
a warning was given
By this man about whom the chroniclers persist in reporting that for
a purpose that eludes them
270   He was dressed in white about this man who of course won't be
found
Then the fall of a lance against a helmet here the musician wrought
marvels
All reason goes away[24] when the hour could be struck without your
being there

In the shadows of the stage set the people are admitted to
contemplate the great feasts
One always very much likes to see eating on stage
275   From the inside of the pâté crowned with pheasants
Dwarfs black on one side and rainbow on the other raise the lid
To spread out in trappings of little bells and laughs
A burst *in contrast* of traces of shots fired of the revolving crust
Dissolve to the Ardents' ball[25] *blurred flashback* to the episode which
closely follows that of the stag

280   Un homme peut-être trop habile descend du haut des tours de
        Notre-Dame[26]
        En voltigeant sur une corde tendue
        Son balancier de flambeaux leur lueur insolite au grand jour
        Le buisson des cinq sauvages dont quatre captifs l'un de l'autre le
        soleil de plumes[27]
        Le duc d'Orléans prend la torche la main la mauvaise main
285   Et quelque temps après[28] à huit heures du soir la main
        On s'est toujours souvenu qu'elle jouait avec le gant
        La main le gant une fois deux fois *trois fois*
        Dans l'angle sur le fond du palais le plus blanc les beaux traits ambi-
        gus de Pierre de Lune[29] à cheval
        Personnifiant le second luminaire
290   *Finir* sur l'emblème de la reine en pleurs[30]
        Un souci[31] Plus ne m'est rien rien ne m'est plus

                                                 Oui sans toi
        Le soleil

                               Marseille, décembre 1940

280   A man perhaps too skilled descends from the top of the towers of
      Notre-Dame[26]
      Balancing on a tightrope
      His pole of torches their odd gleam in broad daylight
      The bush of five savages four of whom are captive of each other the
      sun of feathers[27]
      The Duke of Orleans takes the torch the hand the evil hand
285   And some time later[28] at eight in the evening the hand
      It has always been remembered that it was playing with the glove
      The hand the glove once twice *three times*
      In the corner against the backdrop of the whitest palace the hand-
      some ambiguous features of Pedro de Luna[29] on horseback
      Personifying the second luminary
290   To *end* on the emblem of the queen in tears[30]
      A marigold[31] Nevermore is there aught for me naught is there
      evermore

                               Yes without you

      The sun

Marseilles, December 1940

(JPC)

From 1940–1943 in *Poèmes*

1948

Frôleuse

Mes malles n'ont plus de poids les étiquettes sont des lueurs courant
    sur une mare
Sera-ce assez que tout pour cette contrée où mène bien après sa mise
    au rebut la diligence de nuit
Toute en cristal noir le long des meules tournant de cailles
Château qui tremble et j'en jure que vient de poser devant moi un
    éclair
5   Lieu frustré de tout ce qui pourrait le rendre habitable
Je ne vois qu'étroits couloirs enchevêtrés
Escaliers à vis
Seulement au haut de la tour de guet
Eclate l'air taillé en rose
10   Bannie superstitieusement la place primitive d'une brassée de joncs
    pour s'étendre
L'architecte fou de ce qui restait d'espace libre
Semble avoir rêvé un garage pour mille tables rondes
A chacune d'elles sont présumés souper au caviar au
    champagne
Avec moi des bustes de cire plus beaux les uns que les autres mais
    parmi eux méconnaissable s'est glissé un buste vivant
15   Bustes car il n'y a qu'une nappe à reflets changeants pour toutes les
    tables
Assez lacunaire pour emprisonner la taille de toutes ces femmes
    fausses et vraies
Tout ce qui est ou manque d'être au-dessous de la nappe se dérobe
    dans la musique
Oracle attendu de la navette d'un soulier
Plus brillant qu'un poisson jeté dans l'herbe
20   Ou d'un mollet qui fait un bouquet des lampes de mineur
Ou du genou qui lance un volant dans mon cœur
Ou d'une bouche qui penche qui penche à verser son parfum

Flirt

My trunks have become weightless the stickers are lights flitting
    across a pond
Will it suffice that everything for this region that is reached by the
    night coach long after it has been scrapped
Entirely in black crystal along quail-gyrating millstones
Trembling castle and I swear one that a lightning bolt has just set
    down before me
5   A locality bereft of anything that could make it inhabitable
I only see narrow tangled hallways
Spiral staircases
But atop the watch tower
The rose-hewn air is bursting
10 Superstitiously banished the primitive place of an armful of rushes
    to lie down upon
The architect crazed by the free space remaining
Seems to have dreamed up a garage for a thousand round tables
At each one waxen torsos are presumed to feast with me on caviar
    on champagne
Each torso lovelier than the other but among them unrecognizable a
    living torso has slipped in
15 Torsos there is indeed but one iridescent tablecloth for all the tables
So inadequate as to confine the waists of all those false and true
    women
Everything that is or narrowly misses being below the tablecloth
    slips away into the music
Oracle expected of a shoe shuttling
Brighter than a fish thrown into grass
20 Or of a calf that makes a nosegay from miners' lamps
Or of a knee that shoots a shuttlecock into my heart
Or of a mouth that inclines to pour its fragrance

Ou d'une main d'abord un peu en marge à l'instant même où il
    apparaît qu'elle n'évite pas un rapport d'ailes avec ma main
O ménisques
25 Au-delà de tous les présents permis et défendus
A dos d'éléphants ces piliers qui s'amincissent jusqu'au fil de soie
    dans les grottes
Ménisques adorable rideau de tangence quand la vie n'est plus qu'une
    aigrette qui boit
Et dis-toi qu'aussi bien je ne te verrai plus

Or of a hand at first somewhat apart at the very instant when it
    seems not to avoid a wing-like relationship with my hand
O meniscuses
25   Beyond all allowed and forbidden presents
On elephantback those pillars that taper to a silken thread
    in caves
Meniscuses lovely curtain of tangency when life is but a drinking
    egret
And you might as well know that besides I shall not see you any
    more

(JPC)

Passage à niveau

D'un coup de baguette ç'avaient été les fleurs
Et le sang
Le rayon se posa sur la fenêtre gelée
Personne
5   Pfff on comprit que l'espace se débondait
Puis l'oreiller d'air s'est glissé sous le sainfoin
Les avalanches ont dressé la tête
Et à l'intérieur des pierres des épaules se sont soulevées
Les yeux étaient encore fermés dans l'eau méfiante
10   Des profondeurs montait la triple collerette
Qui allait faire l'orgueil de l'armoire
Et la chanson des cigales prenait son billet
A la gare encore enveloppée de tous ses fils
La femme mordait une pomme de vapeur[1]
15   Sur les genoux d'une grande bête blanche
Dans les ateliers sur les établis silencieux
Le rabot de la lune lissait les feuilles coupantes
Et la meule crachait ses papillons
Sur la bordure du papier où j'écris

Grade Crossing

With one wave of the wand it had been flowers
And blood
The ray of light settled on the frozen window
No one
5   Puff it became clear that space was spilling out
Then the air pillow slipped under the sainfoin
The avalanches perked up their heads
And inside the stones shoulders rose up
Eyes were still closed in the mistrustful water
10   From the depths arose the triple collar
That was to become the pride of the wardrobe
And the cicadas' song picked up its ticket
At the station still wrapped in all its strings
The woman was biting into a steam apple[1]
15   On the knees of a large white beast
In the workshops on the silent benches
The moon's plane smoothed out the cutting sheets
And the millstone spit out its butterflies
On the very edge of the paper I am writing on

(MAC)

Premiers transparents

Comment veux-tu voici que les plombs sautent encore une fois
Voici la seiche qui s'accoude d'un air de défi à la fenêtre
Et voici ne sachant où déplier son étincelante grille d'égout
Le clown de l'éclipse tout en blanc
5   Les yeux dans sa poche
Les femmes sentent la noix muscade
Et les principaux pastillés fêtent leur frère le vent
Qui a revêtu sa robe à tourniquet des grands jours
Mandarin à boutons de boussoles folles
10   Messieurs les morceaux de papier se saluent de haut en bas des
    maisons

New York

Transparent Firsts

How do you suppose there go the fuses blown once again
There's the cuttlefish leaning defiantly on its elbows at the window
And there's the clown of eclipse all clothed in white
Not knowing where to unfold his sparkling sewer grate
5   His eyes in his pocket
The women smell of nutmeg
And the principal gumdroppers celebrate their brother the wind
Who has put on his formal tourniquet dress
Mandarin with buttons of disoriented compasses
10   Pieces of paper greet each other from housetop to bottom like
       gentlemen

New York

(JPC)

Plus que suspect

Les chênes sont atteints d'une grave maladie
Ils sèchent après avoir laissé échapper
Dans une lumière de purin au soleil couchant
Toute une cohue de têtes de généraux

More than Suspect

The oaks are stricken by a serious illness
They dry up after having let go
Into the glow of a sump at sunset
A whole throng of generals' heads

(JPC)

Intérieur

Une table servie du plus grand luxe
Démesurément longue
Me sépare de la femme de ma vie
Que je vois mal
5   Dans l'étoile des verres de toutes tailles qui la tient renversée en
    arrière
Décolletée en coup de vent

Interior

A table set with the utmost luxury
Inordinately long
Separates me from the woman of my life
Whom I dimly see
5 In the starburst of variously shaped glasses that keeps her tilted
     backwards
Her neckline plunging in a flash

(JPC)

Guerre

Je regarde la Bête pendant qu'elle se lèche
Pour mieux se confondre avec tout ce qui l'entoure
Ses yeux couleur de houle
A l'improviste sont la mare tirant à elle le linge sale les détritus
5   Celle qui arrête toujours l'homme
La mare avec sa petite place de l'Opéra dans le ventre
Car la phosphorescence est la clé des yeux de la Bête
Qui se lèche
Et sa langue
10   Dardée on ne sait à l'avance jamais vers où
Est un carrefour de fournaises
D'en dessous je contemple son palais
Fait de lampes dans des sacs
Et sous la voûte bleu de roi
15   D'arceaux dédorés en perspective l'un dans l'autre
Pendant que court le souffle fait de la généralisation à l'infini de
    celui de ces misérables le torse nu qui se produisent sur la place
    publique avalant des torches à pétrole dans une aigre pluie de sous
Les pustules de la Bête resplendissent de ces hécatombes de jeunes
    gens dont se gorge le Nombre
Les flancs protégés par les miroitantes écailles que sont les armées
Bombées dont chacune tourne à la perfection sur sa charnière
20   Bien qu'elles dépendent les unes des autres non moins que les coqs
    qui s'insultent à l'aurore de fumier à fumier
On touche au défaut de la conscience pourtant certains persistent à
    soutenir que le jour va naître
La porte j'ai voulu dire la Bête se lèche sous l'aile
Et l'on voit est-ce de rire se convulser des filous au fond d'une
    taverne
Ce mirage dont on avait fait la bonté se raisonne
25   C'est un gisement de mercure
Cela pourrait bien se laper d'un seul coup

War

I watch the Beast as it licks itself
The better to blend into all of its surroundings
Its eyes the color of heavy seas
Unexpectedly are the pond drawing unto itself the dirty linen the
    garbage
5   The one that always stops man
The pond with its little Place de l'Opéra in its belly
Because phosphorescence is the key to the eyes of the Beast
That licks itself
And its tongue
10 Darting one never knows in advance in what direction
Is a plexus of furnaces
From underneath I gaze at its palate
Made of lamps in bags
And under the royal blue vault
15 Of ungilded arches arrayed in perspective one within the other
While the breath runs rampant being made of the infinite
    generalization of one of those bare-chested wretches who
    appear in the public square swallowing kerosene torches in an
    acrid shower of coins
The Beast's pustules are resplendent owing to the immolations of
    young men on which the Number gorges
Its flanks protected by the shimmering scales that armies are
Convex scales each one of which turns perfectly on its pivot
20 Although they depend on each other no less than roosters that jeer at
    each other at dawn from dungheap to dungheap
The default of consciousness is at hand yet some persistently
    maintain that the day will dawn
The door I meant the Beast licks itself under the wing
And some thieves can be seen convulsed is it with laughter in the
    back of a tavern
The mirage alleged to have been goodness is rationalized
25 It's a lode of quicksilver
Such as could be lapped up in one gulp

J'ai cru que la Bête se tournait vers moi j'ai revu la saleté de l'éclair
Qu'elle est blanche dans ses membranes dans le délié de ses bois de
    bouleaux où s'organise le guet
Dans les cordages de ses vaisseaux à la proue desquels plonge une
    femme que les fatigues de l'amour ont parée d'un loup vert
30   Fausse alerte la Bête garde ses griffes en couronne érectile autour
    des seins
J'essaie de ne pas trop chanceler quand elle bouge la queue
Qui est à la fois le carrosse biseauté et le coup de fouet
Dans l'odeur suffocante de cicindèle
De sa litière souillée de sang noir et d'or vers la lune elle aiguise une
    de ses cornes à l'arbre enthousiaste du grief
35   En se lovant avec des langueurs effrayantes
Flattée
La Bête se lèche le sexe je n'ai rien dit

I thought the Beast was turning toward me I saw the filth of the
    lightning once again
How white it is in its membranes in the nimbleness of its birch
    groves where a lookout is being posted
In the riggings of its ships at whose prow a woman is plunging
    whom the exertions of lovemaking have adorned with a green
    mask
30   False alarm the Beast holds its claws in an erectile crown around the
    breasts
I try not to falter too much when it wags its tail
Which is at the same time the beveled coach and the whiplash
In the suffocating smell of the tiger-beetle
From its litter fouled with black blood and gold it sharpens one of
    its horns moonward on the enthusiastic tree of wrongs
35   By coiling itself with fearsome lasciviousness
Flattered
The Beast licks its sex I've said nothing

(JPC)

From *Les Etats Généraux*
[States-General]

1948

Dis ce qui est dessous parle
Dis ce qui commence
Et polis mes yeux qui accrochent à peine la lumière
Comme un fourré que scrute un chasseur somnambule
5   Polis mes yeux fait sauter cette capsule de marjolaine
Qui sert à me tromper sur les espèces du jour
Le jour si c'était lui
Quand passe sur les campagnes l'heure de traire
Descendrait-il si précipitamment ses degrés
10   Pour s'humilier devant la verticale d'étincelles
Qui saute de doigts en doigts entre les jeunes femmes des fermes
    toujours sorcières
Polis mes yeux à ce fil superbe sans cesse renaissant de sa rupture
Ne laisse que lui écarte ce qui est tavelé
Y compris au loin la grande rosace des batailles
15   Comme un filet qui s'égoutte sous le spasme des poissons du
    couchant
Polis mes yeux polis-les à l'éclatante poussière de tout ce qu'ils
    ont vu
Une épaule des boucles près d'un broc d'eau verte
Le matin
Dis ce qui est sous le matin sous le soir
20   Que j'aie enfin l'aperçu topographique de ces poches extérieures aux
    éléments et aux règnes
Dont le système enfreint la distribution naïve des êtres et des choses
Et prodigue au grand jour le secret de leurs affinités
De leur propension à s'éviter ou à s'étreindre
A l'image de ces courants
25   Qui se traversent sans se pénétrer sur les cartes maritimes
Il est temps de mettre de côté les apparences individuelles
    d'autrefois
Si promptes à s'anéantir dans une seule châtaigne de culs de
    mandrilles

◀   224

Say what is underneath speak
Say what begins
And burnish my eyes that just manage to catch the light
Like a thicket into which a sleepwalking hunter peers
5   Burnish my eyes explode this firing cap of marjoram
That serves to mislead me about the kinds of day
The day if that's what it was
When the milking hour passes over the countryside
Would it step down by degrees so precipitously
10 In order to humble itself before the vertical of sparks
That flits from finger to finger between the young women of the
    farms ever witching
Burnish my eyes with this superb thread ceaselessly reborn from its
    broken ends
Leave nothing else disregard what is speckled
Including at a distance the great rose window of battles
15 Like a net dripping beneath the spasm of the fishes at sunset
Burnish my eyes burnish them with the bright dust of all that they
    have seen
A shoulder some curls near a jug of green water
Mornings
Say what is under mornings under evenings
20 That I might at last have a topographical glimpse of those pockets
    outside the elements and the kingdoms
Whose system infringes the naïve distribution of beings and
    things
And lavishes in the full light of day the secret of their affinities
Of their propensity to avoid or to embrace each other In the image
    of those currents
25 That cross but do not penetrate each other on nautical charts
The time has come to set aside the individual appearances of the
    past
So ready to disappear in a single chestnut of mandrill
    arses

D'où les hommes par légions prêts à donner leur vie
Echangent un dernier regard avec les belles toutes ensemble
30   Qu'emporte le pont d'hermine d'une cosse de fève
Mais polis mes yeux
A la lueur de toutes les enfances qui se mirent à la fois dans une
    amande
Au plus profond de laquelle à des lieues et des lieues
S'éveille un feu de forge
35   Que rien n'inquiète l'oiseau qui chante entre les 8
De l'arbre des coups de fouet

Whence men in droves prepared to give up their lives
Exchange one last glance with all the belles together
30   That are carried away by the ermine bridge of a bean pod
But burnish my eyes
In the light of all the childhoods that see themselves mirrored all at
    once in an almond
In whose innermost depths leagues and leagues down
A smithy's fire arises
35   May nothing disturb the bird that sings between the 8s
Of the tree of whiplashes

(JPC)

From *Des épingles tremblantes*
[Of Trembling Pins]
1948

La Lanterne sourde[I]

à Aimé Césaire, Georges Gratiant, René Ménil

Et les grandes orgues c'est la pluie comme elle tombe ici et se par-fume: quelle gare pour l'arrivée en tous sens sur mille rails, pour la man-œuvre sur autant de plaques tournantes de ses express de verre! A toute heure elle charge de ses lances blanches et noires, des cuirasses volant en éclats de midi à ces armures anciennes faites des étoiles que je n'avais pas encore vues. Le grand jour de préparatifs qui peut précéder la nuit de Walpurgis au gouffre d'Absalon! J'y suis! pour peu que la lumière se voile, toute l'eau du ciel pique aussitôt sa tente,[2] d'où pendent les agrès de vertige et de l'eau encore s'égoutte à l'accorder des hauts instruments de cuivre vert. La pluie pose ses verres de lampe autour des bambous, aux bobèches de ces fleurs de vermeil agrippées aux branches par des suçoirs, autour desquelles il n'y a qu'une minute toutes les figures de la danse enseignées par deux papillons de sang. Alors tout se déploie au fond du bol à la façon des fleurs japonaises,[3] puis une clairière s'entrouvre: l'héliotropisme y saute avec ses souliers à poulaine[4] et ses ongles vrillés. Il prend tous les cœurs, relève d'une aigrette la sensitive et pâme[5] la fougère dont la bouche ardente est la roue du temps. Mon œil est une violette fermée au centre de l'ellipse, à la pointe du fouet.

Août 1941

The Dark Lantern[1]

for Aimé Césaire, Georges Gratiant, René Ménil

And the grand organs are rain as it falls here and perfumes itself: what a station for the arrival in all directions on a thousand rails, for the maneuver on so many turntables of its glass express trains! At any moment, it charges forth with its black and white lances, breastplates bursting in noonday flashes on those old suits of armor made of stars I hadn't yet seen. The great day of preparations that can precede the Walpurgis Night in Absalom's abyss! I'm there! If the light but veil itself, then all the water of the sky promptly pricks its tent with mildew,[2] from which the rigging hangs down giddily and water again is dripping to attune it from the lofty instruments of green copper. The rain sets down its lamp glasses around the bamboo stalks, onto the sconces of those vermeil flowers clinging to the branches with their suckers, around which there are but a minute all the figures of the dance taught by two blood butterflies. Everything then unfolds at the bottom of the bowl in the manner of Japanese flowers,[3] whereupon a clearing opens up: heliotropism leaps into it with its crakows[4] and its whorled fingernails. It takes all the hearts, lifts up with a feather the sensitive plant and faints[5] the fern whose ardent curl is the wheel of time. My eye is a violet closed in the center of the ellipsis, at the tip of the whip.

August 1941

(MAC)

From *Xénophiles* [Xenophilia]
1948

La nuit en Haïti les fées noires successives portent à sept centimètres au-dessus des yeux les pirogues du Zambèze, les feux synchrones des mornes,[1] les clochers surmontés d'un combat de coqs et les rêves d'éden qui s'ébrouent effrontément autour de la désintégration atomique. C'est à leurs pieds que Wifredo Lam[2] installe son « vêver »,[3] c'est-à-dire la merveilleuse et toujours changeante lueur tombant des vitraux invraisemblablement ouvragés de la nature tropicale sur un esprit libéré de toute influence et prédestiné à faire surgir de cette lueur les images des dieux. Dans un temps comme le nôtre, on ne sera pas surpris de voir se prodiguer, ici nanti de cornes, le loa Carrefour—Elegguà à Cuba[4]—qui souffle sur les ailes des portes. Témoignage unique et frémissant toujours comme s'il était pesé aux balances des feuilles, envol d'aigrettes au front de l'étang où s'élabore le mythe d'aujourd'hui, l'art de Wifredo Lam fuse de ce point où la source vitale mire l'arbre-mystère, je veux dire l'âme persévérante de la race, pour arroser d'étoiles le DEVENIR qui doit être le mieux-être humain.

Janvier 1946

In Haiti at night successive black fairies bear, at a level seven centimeters above the eyes, Zambesi pirogues, synchronous hilltop[1] fires, cockfight-topped spires and dreams of Eden that stir brazenly round the disintegration of atoms. Here, at their feet, Wifredo Lam[2] installs his "*vêver*,"[3] that is the marvelous and ever-shifting light shed by the unbelievably elaborate stained glass windows of tropical nature upon a spirit free of all influences and predestined to bring forth from that light the images of the gods. In such a time as ours, it will come as no surprise to see abounding the Crossroads loa—Elleguà in Cuba[4]—that blows on the wings of doors, here endowed with horns. Bearing witness as no other and always quivering as if weighed in the balance of leaves, like egrets taking wing from the face of the pond where today's myths are born, the art of Wifredo Lam streams out from the point where life's springwaters reflect the mystery tree, by which I mean the persevering soul of the race, so as to shower with stars the BECOMING that must be human betterment.

January 1946

(JPC)

Korwar[1]

Tu tiens comme pas un
Tu as été pris comme tu sortais de la vie
Pour y rentrer
Je ne sais pas si c'est dans un sens ou dans l'autre que tu ébranles la
    grille du parc
5   Tu as relevé contre ton cœur l'herbe serpentine
Et à jamais bouclé les paradisiers du ciel rauque
Ton regard est extra-lucide
Tu es assis
Et nous aussi nous sommes assis
10   Le crâne encore pour quelques jours
Dans la cuvette de nos traits
Tous nos actes sont devant nous
A bout de bras
Dans la vrille de la vigne de nos petits
15   Tu nous la bailles belle sur l'existentialisme
Tu n'es pas piqué des vers[2]

Korwar[1]

You hold on like no other
You were caught as you came out of life
To re-enter it
I don't know if it's in one direction or in another that you shake the
    garden gate
5   You have raised up to your heart the serpentine grass
And forever curled the birds of paradise in the hoarse sky
Your gaze is clairvoyant
You are seated
And we too are seated
10   The skull for a few more days In the dip of our features
All our acts are before us
At arm's length
In the little ones' vine tendril
15   You are feeding us a line on existentialism
There are no flies on you[2]

(JPC)

Uli[I]

Pour sûr tu es un grand dieu
Je t'ai vu de mes yeux comme nul autre
Tu es encore couvert de terre et de sang tu viens de créer
Tu es un vieux paysan qui ne sait rien
5   Pour te remettre tu as mangé comme un cochon
Tu es couvert de taches d'homme
On voit que tu t'en es fourré jusqu'aux oreilles
Tu n'entends plus
Tu nous reluques d'un fond de coquillage
10   Ta création te dit haut les mains et tu menaces encore
Tu fais peur tu émerveilles

Uli[1]

For sure you are a great god
I have seen you with my eyes as no other
You are still covered with earth and blood you have just created
You are an old farmer who knows nothing
5 In order to recover you have eaten like a pig
You are covered with man-spots
Obviously you have stuffed yourself to the ears
You can hear no more
You are leering at us from the inside of a seashell
10 Your creation is telling you hands up and you are still a threat
You fill all with fear and wonder

(JPC)

Dukduk[I]

La sang ne fait qu'un tour
Quand le dukduk se déploie sur la péninsule de la Gazelle[2]
Et que la jungle s'entrouvre sur cent soleils levants
Qui s'éparpillent en flamants
5   A toutes vapeurs de l'ordalie
Comme une locomotive de femmes nues
Au sortir d'un tunnel de sanglots
Là-haut cône[3]
Gare[4]

Dukduk[1]

Blood runs full circle
When the dukduk fans out across the Gazelle peninsula[2]
And when the jungle opens up onto a hundred rising suns
That scatter as flamingos
5   At the ordeal's full steam
Like a locomotive of naked women
Emerging from a tunnel of sobs
Lay a cone[3]
Station[4]

(JPC)

Tiki[1]

Je t'aime à la face des mers
Rouge comme l'œuf quand il est vert
Tu me transportes dans une clairière
Douce aux mains comme une caille
5   Tu m'appuies sur le ventre de la femme
Comme contre un olivier de nacre
Tu me donnes l'équilibre
Tu me couches
Par rapport au fait d'avoir vécu
10 Avant et après
Sous mes paupières de caoutchouc

Tiki[I]

I love you in the face of seas
Red as an egg when it is green
You carry me into a clearing
Soft to the touch as a quail in hand
5   You lean me on woman's belly
As against a mother-of-pearl olive tree
You give me balance
You lay me down
In relation to having lived
10 Before and after
Beneath my rubber eyelids

(JPC)

Rano Raraku[I]

Que c'est beau le monde
La Grèce n'a jamais existé
Ils ne passeront pas
Mon cheval trouve son picotin dans le cratère
5   Des hommes-oiseaux[2] des nageurs courbes
Volètent[3] autour de ma tête car
C'est moi aussi
Qui suis là
Aux trois quarts enlisé
10   Plaisantant des ethnologues
Dans l'amicale nuit du Sud
Ils ne passeront pas
La plaine est immense
Ceux qui s'avancent sont ridicules
15   Les hautes images sont tombées

1948

Rano Raraku[1]

How lovely the world is
Greece never existed
They shall not pass
My horse finds his peck in the crater
5   Birdmen[2] curved swimmers
Flit[3] around my head for
I too
Am there
Three quarters bogged down
10   Kidding some ethnologists
In the friendly Southern night
They shall not pass
The plain is immense
Those who move forward are ridiculous
15   The high images are fallen

1948

(JPC)

From *Oubliés* [Forgotten]

1948

Ecoute au coquillage[1]

Je n'avais pas commencé à te voir tu étais AUBE[2]

Rien n'était dévoilé
Toutes les barques se berçaient sur le rivage
Dénouant les faveurs (tu sais) de ces boîtes de dragées
5   Roses et blanches entre lesquelles ambule une navette d'argent
Et moi je t'ai nommée Aube en tremblant

Dix ans après
Je te retrouve dans la fleur tropicale
Qui s'ouvre à minuit
10   Un seul cristal de neige qui déborderait la coupe de tes deux mains
On l'appelle à la Martinique la *fleur du bal*
Elle et toi vous vous partagez le mystère de l'existence
Le premier grain de rosée devançant de loin tous les autres follement
    irisé contenant tout

Je vois ce qui m'est caché à tout jamais
15   Quand tu dors dans la clairière de ton bras sous les papillons de tes
    cheveux
Et quand tu renais du phénix de ta source
Dans la menthe de la mémoire
De la moire énigmatique de la ressemblance dans un miroir sans
    fond
Tirant l'épingle de ce qu'on ne verra qu'une fois

20   Dans mon cœur toutes les ailes du milkweed
Frètent ce que tu me dis

Tu portes une robe d'été que tu ne connais pas
Presque immatérielle elle est constellée en tous sens d'aimants en fer
    à cheval d'un beau rouge minium à pieds bleus

Sur mer, 1946

Seashell Sail[I]

I had not begun to see you you were DAWN[2]

Nothing was unfurled
All the boats were rocking on the shore
Unraveling the ribbons (you know) of the boxes of sugared almonds
5   Pink and white ones between which a silver shuttle ambulates
And trembling I named you Dawn

Ten years later
I find you again in the tropical flower
That opens at midnight
10   A single crystal of snow that would run over the cup of both your
         hands
It is called the *flower of the ball* in Martinique
It shares with you the mystery of existence
The first bead of dew far ahead of all the others wildly iridescent
         encompassing all

I see what is forever hidden from me
15   When you sleep in the clearing of your arm under the butterflies of
         your hair
And when you are reborn from the phoenix of your fountainhead
In the mint of memory
Of enigmatic moire of resemblance in a fathomless mirror
Pulling chestnuts from what will be seen only once

20   In my heart all the milkweed wings Lade what you tell me
You are wearing a summer dress that you do not know

Almost insubstantial it is star-spangled in all directions with mag-
         nets shaped like horseshoes in lovely minium red with blue feet

At sea, 1946

(JPC)

Sur la route de San Romano[I]

La poésie se fait dans un lit comme l'amour
Ses draps défaits sont l'aurore des choses
La poésie se fait dans les bois

Elle a l'espace qu'il lui faut
5   Pas celui-ci mais l'autre que conditionnent
    L'œil du milan
    La rosée sur une prèle
    Le souvenir d'une bouteille de Traminer embuée sur un
       plateau d'argent
    Une haute verge de tourmaline sur la mer
10   Et la route de l'aventure mentale
    Qui monte à pic
    Une halte elle s'embroussaille aussitôt

Cela ne se crie pas sur les toits
Il est inconvenant de laisser la porte ouverte
15 Ou d'appeler des témoins

    Les bancs de poissons les haies de mésanges
    Les rails à l'entrée d'une grande gare
    Les reflets des deux rives
    Les sillons dans le pain
20   Les bulles du ruisseau
    Les jours du calendrier
    Le millepertuis

L'acte d'amour et l'acte de poésie
Sont incompatibles
25 Avec la lecture du journal à haute voix

    Le sens du rayon de soleil
    La lueur bleue qui relie les coups de hache du bûcheron
    Le fil du cerf-volant en forme de cœur ou de nasse
    Le battement en mesure de la queue des castors

On the Road to San Romano[I]

Poetry like love is made in a bed like love
Its crumpled sheets are the dawn of things
Poetry is made in the woods

It has the space it needs
5   Not this one but the other shaped by
      The eye of the kite
      The dew on a horsetail
      The memory of a bottle frosted over on a
        silver tray
      A tall rod of tourmaline on the sea
10   And the road of the mental adventure
      That climbs abruptly
      One stop and bushes cover it instantly

That isn't to be shouted from the rooftops
It's improper to leave the door open
15 Or to summon witnesses

      The shoals of fish the hedges of titmice
      The rails at the entrance of a great station
      The reflections of both riverbanks
      The crevices in the bread
20   The bubbles in the stream
      The days of the calendar
      The St. John's wort

The act of love and poetry
Are incompatible
25 With reading a newspaper aloud

      The course of a sunbeam
      The blue light linking the blows of an axe
      The kite string shaped like a heart or hoop net
      The beaver's tails beating in time

30   La diligence de l'éclair
        Le jet de dragées du haut des vieilles marches
        L'avalanche

        La chambre aux prestiges
        Non messieurs ce n'est pas la huitième Chambre
35   Ni les vapeurs de la chambrée un dimanche soir

                Les figures de danse exécutées en transparence au-dessus des
                    mares
                La délimitation contre un mur d'un corps de femme au
                    lancer de poignards
                Les volutes claires de la fumée
                Les boucles de tes cheveux
40   La courbe de l'éponge des Philippines
                Les lacés du serpent corail
                L'entrée du lierre dans les ruines
                Elle a tout le temps devant elle

        L'étreinte poétique comme l'étreinte de chair
45   Tant qu'elle dure
        Défend toute échappée sur la misère du monde

                                                            1948

30   The swiftness of lightning
The casting of candy from the old stairs
The avalanche

The room of marvels
No gentlemen is not courtroom
35 Nor the haze in a roomful of soldiers some Sunday evening

       The figures of a dance transparent above the
          marshes
       The outline on the wall of a woman's body at
          daggerthrow
       The bright spirals of smoke
       The curls of your hair
40   The curve of a Philippine sponge
       The twists of a coral snake
       The ivy into the ruins
       It has all the time it needs

The embrace of poetry like that of the flesh
45 As long as it lasts
Shuts out all the woes of the world

1948

(MAC)

From *Constellations*
1959

Personnages dans la nuit
guidés par les traces
phosphorescentes des escargots[1]

Rares sont ceux qui ont éprouvé le besoin d'une aide semblable en plein jour,—ce plein jour où le commun des mortels a l'aimable prétention de voir clair. Ils s'appellent Gérard, Xavier, Arthur[2] ... ceux qui ont su qu'au regard de ce qui serait à atteindre les chemins tracés, si fiers de leurs poteaux indicateurs et ne laissant rien à désirer sous le rapport du bien tangible appui du pied, ne mènent strictement nulle part. Je dis que les autres, qui se flattent d'avoir les yeux grands ouverts, sont à leur insu perdus dans un bois. A l'éveil, le tout serait de refuser à la fallacieuse clarté le sacrifice de cette lueur de labradorite[3] qui nous dérobe trop vite et si vainement les prémonitions et les incitations du rêve de la nuit quand elle est tout ce que nous avons en propre pour nous diriger sans coup férir dans le dédale de la rue.

Persons in the Night
Guided by
Phosphorescent Snail Tracks[1]

They are few, those who have experienced a need for such help in the full light of day—that same light of day in which the common run of mankind has the amiable pretension of seeing clearly. They are named Gérard, Xavier, Arthur[2] . . . those who have known that in comparison with what could be achieved, the laid-out paths, so proud of their signposts and leaving nothing to be desired as regards their tangible footing, lead exactly nowhere. I say that the others, who congratulate themselves on seeing with wide-open eyes, are unwittingly lost in the woods. Upon awakening, the best thing would be to refuse to sacrifice to fallacious clarity the labradorite's[3] glimmer that robs us too quickly and so vainly of the premonitions and the incitements of night dreams when it is all we have that is ours to guide us unerringly in the maze of streets.

(JPC)

Femmes sur la plage

Le sable dit au liège: « Comme le lit de sa plus belle nuit je moule ses formes qui suspendent en leur centre la navette de la mer. Je la flatte comme un chat, à la démembrer vers tous ses pôles. Je la tourne vers l'ambre, d'où fusent en tous sens les Broadways électriques. Je la prends comme la balle au bond, je l'étends sur un fil, j'évapore jusqu'à la dernière bulle ses lingeries et, de ses membres jetés, je lui fais faire la roue[1] de la seule ivresse d'être. » Et le liège dit au sable: « Je suis la palette de son grain, je creuse le même vertige à la caresse. Je l'abîme et je la sublime,[2] ainsi les yeux mi-clos jusqu'à l'effigie de la déité immémoriale au long du sillage des pierres levées et je vaux ce que pour son amant, la première fois qu'elle s'abandonne, elle pèse dans ses bras. »

Women on the Beach

The sand says to the cork float: "As the bed of her loveliest night I mould her shapes that suspend in their center the shuttle of the sea. I cajole her like a cat, so much as to dismember her to her farthest reaches. I turn her toward the amber, from which electric Broadways flash out in all directions. I take her like a ball on the rebound, I stretch her out on a string, I evaporate her underlinen to the very last bubble and, with her castoff limbs, I make her turn cartwheels[1] in rapt celebration of simply being." And the cork float says to the sand: "I am the paddle of her grain, I tease the same dizzying thrill from a caress. I abase her and I upraise her,[2] thus with eyes half shut to the height of the immemorial deity's effigy along the wake of standing stones and I am equal to what she weighs for her lover in his arms, the first time she gives herself."

(JPC)

Femme à la blonde aisselle
coiffant sa chevelure
à la lueur des étoiles

Qu'y a-t-il entre cette cavité sans profondeur tant la pente en est douce à croire que c'est sur elle que s'est moulé le baiser, qu'y a-t-il entre elle et cette savane déroulant imperturbablement au-dessus de nous ses sphères de lucioles? Qui sait, peut-être le reflet des ramures du cerf dans l'eau troublée qu'il va boire parmi les tournoiements en nappes du pollen et l'amant luge tout doucement vers l'extase. Que sous le pouvoir du peigne cette masse fluide, mûrement brassée de sarrasin et d'avoine, tout au long épinglée de décharges électriques, n'est pas plus confondant dans sa chute le torrent qui bondit couleur de rouille à chaque dé tour du parc du château de Fougères[1] aux treize tours par la grâce du geste qui découvre et recouvre le nid sournoisement tramé des vrilles de la clématite.[2]

Woman with Blond Underarm
Combing her Hair
in the Starlight

What is there between that shallow cavity whose slope is so gentle as to suggest that the kiss modeled itself after it, what is there between it and that savannah imperturbably unraveling above us its firefly spheres? Who knows, perhaps the reflection of the stag's antlers in the troubled water that he goes to drink among the swirling sheets of pollen and the lover very gently sleighs toward ecstasy. Than under the comb's sway this fluid mass, mellow-brewed with buckwheat and oats, pinned throughout with electrical discharges, is no more mingling in its fall the leaping rust-colored torrent at every turn of the grounds of the château of Fougères[1] with its thirteen towers by the grace of the gesture that uncovers and covers over the slyly woven nest of the clematis's tendrils.[2]

(JPC)

L'Etoile matinale

Elle dit au berger: « Approche. C'est moi qui t'attirais enfant vers ces caves profondes où la mer en se retirant gare les œufs des tempêtes que lustre le varech, aux myriades de paupières baissées. Seulement à la lumière frisante,[1] comme on met la main sur les superbes fossiles au long de la route qui se cherche dans la montagne dynamitée, tu brûlais de voir jaillir l'arête d'un coffre de très ancien ouvrage qui contînt (ce n'est même pas la peine de le forcer) tout ce qui peut ruisseler d'aveuglant au monde. Je te le donne *parce que c'est toi* comme chaque jour pour que tes sillons grisollent[2] et que, plus flattée qu'aucune, ta compagne sourie en te retrouvant. »

Morning Star

It says to the shepherd: "Come nearer. When you were a child I drew you toward those deep caves where the retreating sea stores up the eggs of tempests polished by kelp, with its myriad of closed eyelids. Only in the glancing[1] light, as the hand takes the superb fossils along the road that seeks itself out in the dynamited mountain, you longed ardently to see spring forth the spine of a coffer crafted long ago that contained (it's not even necessary to force it open) every dazzling thing that can stream out in the world. I give it to you *because it's you* as is every day, so that your furrows may warble[2] and that, flattered more than anyone, your companion might smile at finding you again."

(MAC)

Personnage blessé

L'homme tourne toute la vie autour d'un petit bois cadenassé dont il ne distingue que les fûts noirs d'où s'élève une vapeur rose. Les souvenirs de l'enfance lui font à la dérobée croiser la vieille femme que la toute première fois il en a vu sortir avec un très mince fagot d'épines incandescentes. (Il avait été fasciné en même temps qu'il s'était entendu crier, puis ses larmes par enchantement s'étaient taries au scintillement du bandeau de lin qu'aujourd'hui il retrouve dénoué dans le ciel.) Cette lointaine initiation le penche malgré lui sur le fil des poignards[1] et lui fait obsessionnellement caresser cette balle d'argent que le comte Potocki[2] passe pour avoir polie des saisons durant à dessein de se la loger dans la tête. Sans savoir comment il a bien pu y pénétrer, à tout moment l'homme peut s'éveiller à l'intérieur du bois en douce chute libre d'ascenseur au Palais des Mirages entre les arbres éclairés du dedans dont vainement il tentera d'écarter de lui une feuille cramoisie.

Injured Person

Man circles all his life around a small padlocked wood where he only distinguishes the black boles from which a pink vapor rises. The memories of childhood make him furtively pass the old woman that he saw the very first time emerging from it with a slender bundle of incandescent thorns. (He had been fascinated all the while he had heard himself cry out, then his tears as by enchantment had dried with the scintillation of the linen blindfold that today he rediscovers undone in the sky.) That distant initiation makes him lean in spite of himself over the daggers' edge[1] and makes him obsessively stroke the silver bullet that Count Potocki[2] is reputed to have polished for many a season with the intention of lodging it in his skull. Without knowing how he was able to enter it, at any time man can wake up inside the wood in a gentle elevator free fall in the Palace of Mirages among trees lit from within of which he will vainly attempt to brush aside a crimson leaf.

(JPC)

Le Chant du rossignol à minuit
et la pluie matinale

La clé de sol enjambe la lune. Le criocère[1] sertit la pointe de l'épée du sacre. Un voilier porté par les alizés s'ouvre une passe dans les bois. Et les douze gouttes du philtre s'extravasent en un flot de sève qui emparadise les cœurs et feint de dégager cette merveille (on ne peut que l'entrevoir) qui, du côté bonheur, ferait contrepoids au sanglot. Les chères vieilles croches tout embrasées reposent le couvercle de leur marmite.

The Song of the Nightingale at Midnight and the Morning Rain

The treble clef steps over the moon. The crioceris[1] sets the tip of the anointing sword in a bezel. A sailboat borne by tradewinds clears a channel through the woods for itself. And the twelve drops of the philtre extravasate in a flow of sap that imparadises the heart and feigns to release that wonder (it can only be glimpsed) which, as far as happiness is concerned, would countervail a sob. The dear old quavers all aflame put their pot-cover back.

(JPC)

Le Réveil au petit jour

A tire-d'aile s'éloigne le bonnet de la meunière et voilà qu'il survole le clocher, repoussant les cerfs-volants[1] de la nuit, comme les autres en forme de cœurs et de cages. La charrue à tête d'alouette le contemple de l'herbe grasse. Au diapason de tout ce qui s'étire au-dehors, une dernière flamme se cambre au centre du lit frais défait. En contrepoint. dans le murmure qui s'amplifie s'essore une barcarolle dont jaillit tintinnabulant notre grand ami Obéron,[2] qui règne sur le cresson de fontaine. Chut! Sans plus bouger il nous convie à entendre le beau Huon frappe à la fois aux Cent Portes. En effet le cor magique brame[3] en chandelier dans le lointain. Le sang coulera mais il ne sera pas dit que le Chevalier manque à nous rapporter les quatre molaires et les moustaches[4] aux prix desquelles est Esclarmonde et s'accomplit le sacrifice quotidien.

The Awakening at Daybreak

Fleet-winged the bonnet of the miller's wife flies away and there it is passing over the steeple, repelling the kites[1] of night, like the others in the shape of hearts and cages. The lark-headed plough gazes upon it from the lush grass. In tune with all that stretches outdoors, a last flame arches in the center of the freshly unmade bed. In counterpoint, within the increasing murmur a barcarole is soaring, from which our great friend Oberon,[2] who lords over the fountain cress, springs out tintinnabulating. Shh! Without moving any longer he bids us hear handsome Huon knocking at the Hundred Doors all at once. And the magic horn indeed troats[3] chandelier-like in the distance. Blood will flow but it shall not be said that the Knight fails to bring back to us the four molars and the mustaches[4] for which the prize is Esclarmonde and the consummation of the daily sacrifice.

(JPC)

Femmes au bord d'un lac à la surface irisée par le passage d'un cygne

Leur rêverie se veloute de la chair d'une pensée proportionnée aux dimensions de l'œil cyclopéen qu'ouvrent les lacs et dont la fixité fascina qui devait se faire le terrible héraut du Retour Eternel. Le beau sillage partant du cœur innerve les trois pétales de base de l'immense fleur qui vogue se consumant sans fin pour renaître dans une flambée de vitraux. Ce sont les oratoires sous-jacents, plus que profanes, où se retirent les belles, chacune dans son secret. Elles s'y rendent[1] en tapis volant, sur le merveilleux nuage d'inconnaissance. C'est là que la vapeur des alambics fait ruche[2] et que le bras, qui reflète à s'y méprendre le col de cygne, pointe tout distraitement sur l'angle du miel. Plus, entre les mots, la moindre brise: le luxe est dans la volupté.[3]—Toute femme est la Dame du Lac.

Women by the Shore of a Lake
Made Iridescent by a Passing Swan

Their reverie softens like the velvety flesh of a thought proportioned to the dimensions of the cyclopean eye that the lakes open and whose spellbinding steady stare was to become the terrible harbinger of the Eternal Return. The beautiful wake stemming from the heart innervates the three base petals of the immense seafaring flower wasting away endlessly the better to revive in a blaze of stained glass. They are the subjacent, more than unhallowed oratories to which the belles with-draw, each bearing her own secret. They arrive[1] there by flying carpet, on the marvelous cloud of unknowing. It is there that the retorts' vapor makes hive[2] and that the arm, the mirror image of a swan's neck, points quite absentmindedly to the honey's angle. No longer, between words, the slightest breeze: luxury lies in voluptuous delight.[3]—Every woman is the Lady of the Lake.

(JPC)

Le Bel Oiseau déchiffrant l'inconnu
au couple d'amoureux

Les bancs des boulevards extérieurs s'infléchissent avec le temps sous l'étreinte des lianes qui s'étoilent tout bas de beaux yeux et de lèvres. Alors qu'ils nous paraissent libres continuent autour d'eux à voleter et fondre les unes sur les autres ces fleurs ardentes. Elles sont pour nous traduire en termes concrets l'adage des mythographes qui veut que l'attraction universelle soit une qualité de l'espace et l'attraction charnelle la fille de cette qualité mais oublie par trop de spécifier que c'est ici à la fille, pour le bal, de parer la mère. Il suffit d'un souffle pour libérer ces myriades d'aigrettes porteuses d'akènes. Entre leur essor et leur retombée selon la courbe sans fin du désir s'inscrivent en harmonie tous les signes qu'englobe la partition céleste.

The Lovely Bird Deciphering the Unknown for a Pair of Lovers

The benches of the outer boulevards bend down in time under the embrace of vines that light up softly in a spangle of beautiful eyes and lips. While they appear vacant to us, around them those ardent flowers continue to flutter and infuse each other. They are to translate in concrete terms the adage of mythographers according to which the gravitational pull of heavenly bodies is allegedly a characteristic of space and carnal desire the daughter of that characteristic but which altogether forgets to specify that it is up to the daughter, for the ball, to adorn the mother. A single breath is sufficient to set free those myriads of egrets bearing achenes. Between their upward and their downward flight along the endless curve of desire all the signs encompassed by the celestial score are set down in harmony.

(JPC)

From *Le La*
[The Tone Setting]
1961

La « dictée de la pensée » (ou d'autre chose?) à quoi le surréalisme a voulu originellement se soumettre et s'en remettre à travers l'écriture dite « automatique, » j'ai dit à combien d'aléas dans la vie de veille son écoute (active-passive) était exposée. D'un immense prix, par suite, m'ont toujours été ces phrases ou tronçons de phrases, bribes de monologue ou de dialogue extraits du sommeil et retenus sans erreur possible tant leur articulation et leur intonation demeurent nettes au réveil—réveil qu'ils semblent produire car on dirait qu'ils viennent tout juste d'être proférés. Pour sibyllins qu'ils soient, chaque fois que je l'ai pu je les ai recueillis avec tous les égards dus aux pierres précieuses. Il fut un temps où je les enchâssais tout bruts au départ d'un texte (« le Message automatique »[1] et quelques autres). Je m'imposais par là d'« enchaîner » sur eux, fût-ce dans un tout autre registre, à charge d'obtenir que ce qui allait suivre *tînt* finalement auprès d'eux et participât de leur très haut degré d'effervescence. D'une de ces phrases à allure de sentence particulièrement belle: « Il y aura toujours une pelle au vent dans les sables du rêve, » en 1943 j'ai fait la trame d'un long poème: « les Etats généraux, » qui est sans doute celui auquel je tiens le plus. Même si, à beaucoup près, « la bouche d'ombre »[2] ne m'a pas parlé avec la même générosité qu'à Hugo et s'est même contentée de propos décousus, l'essentiel est qu'elle ait bien voulu me souffler parfois quelques mots qui me demeurent la *pierre de touche,* dont je m'assure qu'ils ne s'adressaient qu'à moi seul (tant j'y reconnais, mais toute limpide et portée à la puissance incantatoire, ma propre voix) et que, si décourageants qu'ils soient pour l'interprétation au pied de la lettre, sur le plan émotif ils étaient faits pour me donner le *la.*

Décembre 1960

The experience (active-passive) of listening to the "dictation of thought" (or of something else?) to which surrealism originally wished to subject itself and subscribe through so-called "automatic" writing is, as I have already stated, exposed to many random occurrences in waking life. They have been immensely valuable, therefore, those sentences or fragments of sentences, scraps of monologue or dialogue extracted from sleep and retained without any possibility of error, so distinct do their articulation and intonation remain at awakening—an awakening that they seem to bring about, for one has the impression that they have just been uttered. However sybilline they might be, on every possible occasion I have collected them with the careful consideration owed to precious stones. There was a time when I mounted them, rough as they were, at the outset of a text ("The Automatic Message"[1] and a few others). I thereby obligated myself to "add on" to them, be it in an entirely different register, on condition that what followed would ultimately *hold up* in their proximity and would partake of their very high degree of effervescence. From one of those particularly beautiful maxim-like sentences: "In the sands of dreams there will always be a spade in the wind," in 1943 I made the thread of a long poem, "The States-General," which is without doubt the one I value the most. Even if, by a wide margin, the "mouth of shadows"[2] did not speak to me with the same generosity as it did to Hugo and was even content to make desultory remarks, what matters is that it was willing to suggest to me some words that remain for me a *touchstone*, words that I assure myself were intended for me alone (so surely do I recognize in them, albeit crystal clear and raised to an incantatory power, my own voice) and that, as discouraging as they may be as far as a to-the-letter interpretation is concerned, on an emotional plane they were made to set the tone for me.

December 1960

(JPC)

NOTES

(Works cited are by Breton except as otherwise indicated. Publication data are given in notes only for works not included in Selected Bibiliography)

Preface

1. Reverdy's original statement is in Pierre Reverdy, *Nord-Sud* (Paris, 1918):

> The image is a pure creation of the mind.
> It cannot be born from a comparison but from a juxtaposition of two more or less distant realities.
> The more the relationship between the two juxtaposed realities is distant and true, the stronger the image will be—and its emotional power and poetic reality.

Breton picks it up in his *First Surrealist Manifesto* and claims to go beyond it, for Reverdy, he says, is judging the image a posteriori as it is already, whereas the surrealists will create it (see *Manifestoes of Surrealism*, p. 20). It is also in this *Manifesto* that Breton discusses the "man soluble in his thought."

2. Quoted in Henri Béhar's introduction to the *Œuvres complètes* of Tristan Tzara (Paris: Flammarion, 1975), vol. I.

3. For Breton's theory of man soluble in his thought, see *First Surrealist Manifesto* and also Mary Ann Caws, *André Breton*, p. 25.

4. This line from "Sur la route qui monte et descend" [On the Road Climbing and Descending] (in *Le Revolver à cheveux blancs)* provides an illustration of the transfer of images, while the baroque is seen as neighbor to the surrealist vision, as discussed in the chapter "From Designation to Contemplation" in Mary Ann Caws, *The Eye in the Text: Essays on Perception, Mannerist to Modern* (Princeton: Princeton University Press, 1981).

5. « On me dit que là-bas » [They tell me that over there] (in *L'Air de l'eau*, pp. 158–159).

6. For some discussion of the interchange and development between Dada and surrealism, see Mary Ann Caws, *The Poetry of Dada and Surrealism.*

7. The mirror image here, with the woman combing her hair, takes us back to the long tradition of the poetic celebration of the beauty of feminine tresses, especially by Baudelaire, Mallarmé, and then Apollinaire, Aragon, Desnos, Leiris, to the present. See on this point Richard Stamelman, "Relational Structures of Surrealist Poetry," *Dada/Surrealism*, no. 6 (1976), and the chapter "For a Cinema of the Central Eye" in Caws, *The Eye in the Text.*

8. See also Robert Desnos' haunting image of the mermaid, in many points similar to this one: Melusina takes many forms but sings enduringly in the surrealist mind. On Melusina, see especially Wallace Fowlie, *The Age of Surrealism* (Bloomington: University of Indiana Press, 1960). For one of the best discussions of the imagery and imagination of surrealism, see Ferdinand Alquié, *The Philosophy of Surrealism*.

9. *Arcane 17*, p. 60.

10. "Monsieur V," in *Mont de piété*, pp. 44–45.

Introduction: The Poethics of André Breton

1. *Entretiens*, p. 139. All translations are mine.

2. « Entretien avec Roger Vitrac: André Breton n'écrira plus, » *Journal du peuple*, April 7, 1923. Quoted by Marguerite Bonnet, *André Breton: Naissance de l'aventure surréaliste*, p. 281n.

3. *Manifestes du surréalisme*, pp. 53–54.

4. Sigmund Freud, "Die Traumdeutung," in *Gesammelte Werke*, vols. 2–3 (London: Imago Publishing Co., 1942), p. 323. The influence of Freudian psychoanalysis on Breton has been shown to be quite limited. Indeed, in many respects, Breton's views run counter to Freud's. The latter does not lend credence to so-called premonitory dreams or to the phenomenon of "déjà vu." Furthermore, where for Breton the reality principle and the pleasure principle converge, indeed coincide, in the exercise and fulfillment of desire, they cannot meet according to Freud. The demystifying process of psychoanalysis clearly reflects a positivistic ethic, and is based on the assumption that the Id is to be tamed, that its energies are best channeled into rational modes of behavior. For Freud, repression is not an evil, but a necessity. As regards *dépaysement*, it is to some extent linked to the experience of *das Unheimliche*, "the uncanny," analyzed by Freud in 1919 (see *Gesammelte Werke, vol. 12* [London: Imago Publishing Co., 1947], pp. 227–268).

5. *Entretiens*, pp. 153–154.

6. « Francis Picabia, » in *Les Pas perdus*, p. 135.

7. « Signe ascendant," in *La Clé des champs*, p. 133.

8. « Lettre aux voyantes, » in *Manifestes du surréalisme*, p. 233.

9. *L'Amour fou*, pp. 12–13.

10. Ibid., Chapter 1.

11. « Lettre à A. Rolland de Renéville » (1932), in *Point du jour*, p. *99*.

12. « Picasso dans son élément, » in *Point du jour*, pp. 145–146.

13. Jungian psychology offers many more affinities with Breton than does Freud's, despite Breton's seeming unfamiliarity with, and perhaps deliberate ignorance of, Jung's work.

14. "Introduction aux 'Contes bizarres' d'Achim d'Arnim," in *Point du jour*, p. 143.

15. *L'Amour fou*, p. *14*.

16. Isidore Ducasse (pseud. Lautréamont), *Les Chants de Maldoror*, in *(Œuvres complètes* (Paris: Garnier-Flammarion, 1969), p. 203.

17. Ibid., p. 234.

18. *Point du jour*, p. 142.

19. *Point du jour*, p. 182.

20. "En marge des *Champs magnétiques.* Le Groupe. La Rupture," *Change* 7 (1970): 9–29.

21. "Le Message automatique,» in *Point du jour,* p. 165.

22. Ibid., pp. 185–186.

23. « Les Mots sans rides,» in *Les Pas perdus,* p. 141.

24. « Crise de l'objet,» in *Point du jour,* p. 130; « Manifeste du surréalisme,» in *Manifestes du surréalisme,* p. 33·

25. « Introduction au Discours sur le peu de réalité,» in *Point du jour, pp.* 22–23.

26. « Du surréalisme dans ses œuvres vives,» in *Manifestes du surréalisme,* p. 357. For a discussion of surrealist prosody and syntax, see J. H. Matthews, "Grammar, Prosody, and French Surrealist Poetry," *Dada/Surrealism,* no. 9 (1979): 83–97; J. Gratton, "Runaway: Textual Dynamics in the Surrealist Poetry of André Breton," *Forum for Modern Language Studies,* XVIII, no 2 (1982): 126–144.

27. T. S. Eliot, "The Metaphysical Poets," in *Selected Essays* (London: Faber and Faber, 1951), p. 289.

28. *Point du jour,* p. 23.

29. Ibid.

30. *Manifestes du surréalisme,* p. 54.

31. « Flagrant délit,» in *La Clé des champs,* p. 164.

32. *Point du jour,* p. 96.

33. Rosmarie Waldrop, *Against Language? "Dissatisfaction with Language" as Theme and as Impulse Toward Experiments in Twentieth Century Poetry* (The Hague and Paris: Mouton, 1971), pp. 101–111.

34. *L'Amour fou,* p. 116. There is of course no exact English equivalent for such constructions with *à.* Concerning Roussel, see *How I Wrote Certain of My Books,* translated, with notes and a bibliography, by Trevor Winkfield; with two essays on Roussel by John Ashbery (New York: Sun Press, 1977).

35. *La Clé des champs,* p. 133.

36. Ibid., p. 165.

NOTES TO THE POEMS

Age

1. One of the more Rimbaldian of Breton's early verses: compare with Rimbaud's *Aube* [Dawn], for instance.

2. Also a stack of hay and a manure pile: typical surrealist contrast of beauty and its opposite in a startling opposition.

3. Phonetic play on *au secours*, "help!" Literally, someone is shaking an unspecified thing, since *secouer is* a transitive verb.

4. *Plaisanté:* the bed is also made agreeable *(plaisant)* with foliage, to mark the wedding day; the undercurrent of mockery in the verb *plaisanter* [to tease] reverberates here.

For Lafcadio

1. A reference to the nonconformist hero (or antihero) of André Gide's *Les Caves du Vatican* (1914; translated as *Lafcadio's Adventures),* and also to Breton's irreverent, surrealistic friend Jacques Vaché, who showed Breton the initial draft of a projected work on Lafcadio in June 1917 (see « La Confession dédaigneuse, » in *Les Pas perdus,* p. *).*

2. *MAM* can be interpreted as the name of a store or as *a diminutif* [nickname] of *Madame* (besides suggesting *maman,* "Mama"); *VIVier,* as a surname or as a fish-breeding pond. *MAM* and VIV are also linked by a degree of visual symmetry.

3. Vaché was fond of referring to the young woman with whom he lived, Louise, as « ma maîtresse, » although their relationship purportedly remained chaste ("La Confession dédaigneuse, » in *Les Pas perdus,* p. 18).

4. This italicized central section is a collage of near-quotations—from Alfred Jarry's *Ubu Roi,* III, 2 (lines 8–9); from Rimbaud's prose poem « Enfance I, » in *Illuminations* (line 10); and from a letter written by Vaché to Théodore Fraenkel, dated June 16, 1917 (in Jacques Vaché, *Lettres de guerre* [Paris: Au Sans Pareil, Collection de *Littérature,* 1919]) (line 12).

5. *Corps accort:* word play on *corps à corps,* "hand-to-hand combat."

6. *L'entrain* [literally, "spirit, liveliness"] echoes *le lent train* in the preceding line.

7. The "indirect contributions" are also those "collected" by the poet in lines 8-12.

8. *Collage* conveys two meanings: the assemblage of seemingly disparate elements, and the "shacking up" or cohabitation of an unmarried couple; in the latter sense, no doubt a reference to Vaché and his companion Louise.

9. *La retraite:* also implied is "retreat," as from battle, or as the evening retreat of troops into their barracks.

Monsieur V

1. « A la place de l'étoile » also refers to the famous star-shaped square of which the Arch of Triumph is the center; normally capitalized, "Place de l'Etoile." It has been renamed Place Charles-de-Gaulle-Etoile.

2. A play on the homophony *mer*, "sea," and *mère*, "mother."

3. Parallels « BERCEUSE, » line 6. Both words echo line 13 of Rimbaud's « Rêve » (much admired by Breton), which line consists of the single capitalized word "VALSE" [waltz]. "MARCHE" also constitutes a sly retort to Valéry, who had urged Breton to write a traditional sonnet with the exhortation, "Marche! c'est à prendre ou à laisser" [Forward! Take it or leave it] (Letter of July 25, 1918, quoted by Marguerite Bonnet, *André Breton: Naissance de l'aventure surréaliste*, p. 137, n. 112).

4. Probably a reference to Pierre Reverdy and the dedicatee, Paul Valéry. Both poets were then exerting divergent influences on Breton. At the time of the poem's composition (June–July 1918), Valéry's "star" was on the decline, Reverdy's on the rise. "Pierre ou Paul" suggests the expression « Je ne sais plus à quel saint me vouer » [I don't know whom (what saint) to swear by, i.e., I don't know which way to turn].

5. *Tirer les rois:* a reference to the custom of passing around the *galette des rois* (Twelfth-Night cake) from which each person takes a piece in the hope of finding the baked-in *fève* [bean], thus becoming *roi de la fève* [king of the bean]. *Tirer* also suggests the meaning of "to fire upon, shoot." The poem's later context *(Rêve de révolutions)* clearly requires that the image of a king be preserved in translation.

An Unsteady House

1. The text is transcribed verbatim from a newspaper article, except for the proper names, which lend an essential element of surprise to an otherwise banal news item (see Louis Aragon, « Lautréamont et nous, » *Les Lettres françaises*, June 1–14, 1967).

2. Pun on *l'espoir* [hope].

3. A fanciful evocation of the poet, who had recently died (November 1918) at the age of thirty-eight.

Cards on the Dunes

1. *Damée:* literally, "crowned," as in checkers, draughts, etc. or "queened," as in chess. In context *(une serviette damée rouge)*, it suggests *damas* and *damier*, that is, damask and checkered cloth.

2. Pastiche of a line by the popular poet-patriot Paul Déroulède (1846–1914): "L'air est pur, la route est large/Le clairon sonne la charge" [The air is pure, the road is wide/The bugle sounds the charge] (« Le Clairon, » in Déroulède *Chants du soldat* [1872]).

3. *Gros vers:* word play on *gros-vert*, a type of grape characterized by its green color and large size.

"It too is the penitentiary . . ."

1. This poem first appeared as the eighth and concluding part of a longer work, *Le Volubilis et Je sais l'hypoténuse* [Morning glory and I Know the Hypotenuse], in the January 1, 1923, issue of *Littérature* and in the original edition of *Clair de terre*. The entire work was originally dedicated to Simone, Breton's first wife. The preceding seven parts were omitted from all subsequent editions, including the 1966 volume of *Clair de terre*.

2. *Peine* (which can mean "punishment" as well as "distress") and *travaux* ("labor" or "work site," line 15) both tie in with the opening image of the *bagne*.

3. See note 2.

Private

1. *Privé:* "private," and also "deprived."

Cinder Blotter

1. Phonetic play on *cœur caché,* "hidden heart." The king's sealed letter *(lettre de cachet)* is the heart but also, in all probability, the poem.

No Paradise Is Lost

1. *Point de refuge:* can also be read as "point of refuge"; suggests the phrase *point de repère,* "landmark."

Straw Silhouette

1. *Dessert* also means "serves," "provides service to" (as for example a train or bus service).

Broken Line

1. *Patiences:* a characteristic play on two meanings, one obvious, the other arcane (= *rumex patientia,* a plant of the dock family).

Sunflower

1. *Tournesol* also designates litmus paper. Written in 1923, this poem assumed an extraordinary significance for its author after May 29, 1934, the date of his first encounter with Jacqueline Lamba. Breton saw the poem as a prefiguration of the encounter; he commented on the coincidental aspects of the text and of real life in Chapter 4 of *L'Amour fou.*

2. Les Halles: the large, central marketplace in Paris, since dismantled.

3. *Chien qui fume* [Smoking Dog]: a famous night spot near the Halles.

4. The Square des Innocents, the Pont au Change (line 14), the rue Gît-le-Cœur (line 15), and the statue of Etienne Marcel (line 29) are all within walking distance of the site of the Halles.

"Night of filth, night of flowers .."

1. *Râles:* literally, "death rattles." A *râle* is also a bird (a rail or crake).

2. The kite is held back by *strings* but also by *sons (des fils* in both senses). Rather than string out the metaphor, better sacrifice the word play.

3. The continuity of *tree* to *arborescent* is clear in English, but the image *prendre la bourse*—*to* steal the purse—may not be; thus the "taking one thing with another," in the hope of a relatively rich echo of a purse.

4. *Tu me tues* is a necessarily lost word play, so the translation takes the assassination lightly, as a whimsical analogy.

5. *Balai* means "broom" (for sweeping); *genêt* is "broom" (the plant). We have tried to capitalize on this.

6. The succor of the Virgin is not present in the French *chicorée,* but since other plays are lost, we use this variant form of "chicory."

7. *Manchettes* are also newspaper headlines—thus, the headlines dealing with criminals, the cuffs on which those spurts of ink have left dark traces, and so on.

8. *Cheveux de poule* is reminiscent of *chair de poule,* "goose pimples."

9. Really the finger, as in "lay a finger on his lips," but the ritual is not displeasing, so the literal translation is kept: to lay hands upon, hoping also to send the reader back to the assassins.

Free Union

1. The title suggests not only "free love" but also the poem's structural principle: the free association of metaphors.

2. *Fêne,* usually spelled *faîne.* The altered spelling results from the association with *hêtre* (beech tree). The word *fêne* itself is suggested by *foin coupé,* "mown hay" (line 19), the term for "hay-making" being *fenaison.* Last but not least, a common variety of marten is the *martre des hêtres* (beech marten).

3. *Scalare,* usually spelled *scalaire* in French, designates the angelfish *(Pterophyllum scalare)* and the wentletrap, a mollusk of the genus *Scalaria* or *Epitonium.*

4. The technical expression *fusée à mouvement d'horlogerie* (mechanical time fuse) is here exploded. The images of the *fusée* and the *mouvements d'horlogerie* relate to *jambes* (legs), no longer to each other.

5. *Initiales:* besides the more usual meaning, a botanical term designating meristematic cells, also known as initials, viz., fast-multiplying cells at the tips of roots and branches.

6. *Calfats:* not the more common meaning of "ship caulkers," but birds of the weaver finch family (Estrilidae), *Padda or Munia oryzivora,* handsome, finely feathered pink, grey, and black birds often kept in cages.

7. *Orge imperlé:* a coinage derived from the usual *orge perlé,* "pearl barley."

The Verb To Be

1. Play on *ce n'est pas la mer à boire,* "you're not being asked to drink the sea," i.e., it's easier than it looks, that's not asking too much.

2. Reference to the custom of determining whether a person is alive or dead by placing a mirror to his nose and mouth, to observe whether it mists over or not.

3. The adjectives *longs* and *grêles* inflect the meaning of *étonnement* (usually "astonishment") to its more unusual one, i.e., "fissure," "crack" (in a building).

The Forest in the Axe

1. The original French sentence is a multiple word play, the literal rendering of which would be meaningless: *pour des prunes*, "for naught, in vain"; *prunes à l'eau-de-vie*, "brandied plums."

2. Reference to a popular vaudeville play by Eugène Labiche, first performed in 1851 and a repertory piece of the Comédie Française.

3. *Aéré mort is* pitted antithetically against *enterré vivant*, "buried alive."

Knot of Mirrors

1. In *L'Amour fou*, Chapter 1 (pp. 16–17), Breton designates crystal as the perfect expression of creation and spontaneous action. « Nul plus haut enseignement artistique ne me paraît pouvoir être reçu que du cristal. L'œuvre d'art, au même titre d'ailleurs que tel fragment de la vie humaine considérée dans sa signification la plus grave, me paraît dénuée de valeur si elle ne présente pas la dureté, la rigidité, la régularité, le lustre sur toutes ses faces extérieures, intérieures, du cristal. » [No higher artistic message can be conveyed than that of crystal. The work of art, just as any fragment of human life considered in terms of its most meaningful implications, seems to me devoid of value if it does not present the hardness, the rigidity, the regularity, the luster of crystal on all its exterior and interior facets.] See also Introduction, p. 18.

2. The pharmaceutical formula for treatment of angina pectoris.

Postman Cheval

1. Ferdinand Cheval, a rural postman who singlehandedly erected a *palais idéal* between 1879 and 1912 in Hauterives, a small town in the Drôme region, using pebbles and stones that he picked up along country roads after his rounds and cemented together. The structure, totally nonfunctional and extravagantly ornate, attracted the surrealists, who pronounced its creator one of their heroes. Breton called Cheval "le maître incontesté de l'architecture et de la sculpture médianimiques" [the uncontested master of mediumistic architecture and sculpture] in « Le Message automatique » (1933).

2. The image of a locomotive trapped in the jungle most strikingly illustrates the notion of *beauté convulsive* (see Introduction).

3. A reference to an ingenious mechanical duck devised by Jacques de Vaucanson in 1713, a significant date for Breton, who was struck by its analogous configuration to his own initials as he was wont to write them in cursive capital letters ($\mathit{1\!\!/\!\!3}$). (See "« Du poème-objet, » in *Le Surréalisme et la peinture*, p. 265.)

Curtain Curtain

1. *Siffler* instead of the expected *souffler*, "to prompt"; hence the role reversal: catcalls and hisses are heard from the prompter's box.

2. *Un kiosque de glaces* inevitably suggests an ice cream vending stand *(kiosque à glace).*

The Vertebral Sphinx

1. Drops of glass formed by dropping molten glass into water. An example of *beauté convulsive* (see Introduction).

2. In context, *balancier* also suggests other meanings: the handle of a blacksmith's bellows and a mechanical piece with a to-and-fro motion as referred to in line 16.

Vigilance

1. A well-known Paris landmark, of particular significance to the surrealists owing to its associations with late medieval alchemists. In Chapter 4 of *L'Amour fou*, Breton refers to the Tour Saint-Jacques as "the world's great monument to the unrevealed."

Unconscious

1. Suggested by the title are other meanings: unacquainted, unconsummated (without carnal knowledge), unknown.

2. The Porte Saint-Martin, an arch erected in 1674 and bestriding the rue Saint-Martin.

3. *Broyer de la craie,* "to pound chalk," is a reverse image of the idiomatic phrase *broyer du noir,* "to have the blues" (literally, "to grind black").

4. Boron burns with a yellow flame.

5. This line syntactically follows and completes line 51.

A Stalk of Nettle Enters through the Window

1. A European fresh-water cyprinoid fish.

Deadly Rescue

1. The author of *Les Chants de Maldoror,* whom Breton designated as "le grand serrurier de la vie moderne » [the great unlocker of modern life] *(La Clé des champs,* p. 11).

2. A genus of lizard that includes the Gila monster.

3. Lautréamont's birthplace.

4. Cf. the famous concluding line of *Nadja:* "La beauté sera CONVULSIVE ou ne sera pas" [Beauty will be CONVULSIVE or will not be at all], and the expanded remarks on convulsive beauty in Chapter 1 of *L'Amour fou,* among which the following: "Les 'beau comme' de Lautréamont constituent le manifeste même de la beauté convulsive" [The 'as lovely as' of Lautréamont constitute the very manifesto of convulsive beauty].

5. *Chiendent:* literally, "couch grass" (a bothersome weed), and, colloquially, "annoyance, nuisance."

"World in a kiss"

1. The axolotl is a larval salamander from Mexico.

2. *Voie de fait:* à juridical term meaning an act of violence.

3. *Coreopsis:* plant of the thistle family.

4. Perhaps suggested by the South American Orejones Indians, known as the Oreillons in French.

5. A species of water beetle.

6. *Scolopendre is* both an entomological and a botanical term, referring to the centipede (scolopendra) and hart's-tongue (scolopendrium).

"Dreaming I see you . . ."

1. *La rose des vents:* "the rose of winds"—that is, the design on the dial of a mariner's compass showing the thirty-two rhumbs or directions.

2. Shiva, one of the principal gods of Hinduism, identified with the Vedic god Rudra and, as such, the god of destruction. He is worshipped in the form of the *lingam,* or symbolic phallus. As a yoga he is portrayed as seated deep in meditation, holding a trident, a snake coiled around his neck, his body smeared with ashes, and his hair long and matted. As Nataraja, Lord of the Cosmic Dance, he is depicted with four arms, bearing various emblems, and dancing on one foot on a prostrate demon.

"The Marquis de Sade has gone back inside .."

1. Literally, "the Virgin's thread"; *les fils de la Vierge* (plural) is the usual French expression for gossamer.

"Zinnia-red eyes . . ."

1. Grateful acknowledgement for this rendering of *zinzolins* is due Bill Zavatsky and Zack Rogow. (See « André Breton: *The Air of the Water,"* Sun 4, no. 3 [Winter 1979–1980] : 266.)

2. Jacqueline Lamba, whom Breton met in May 1934 and married in August of the same year. The aquatic or marine imagery evident here and in other poems of *Airwater* takes on particular significance in the light of Breton's comment (in connection with « Tournesol, » see *L'Amour fou,* Chapter 4) that Jacqueline played a part as a swimmer in a music-hall show. Intriguing in this context is the letter X, by which Breton designates at the end of *Nadja* a woman—Suzanne Musard—with whom he had a liaison after separating from Simone, his first wife, and before his encounter with the "scandalously beautiful" Jacqueline.

"It was about to be five in the morning"

1. *Ondine:* a reference to an episode related in the concluding part of Chapter 1 of *L'Amour fou.* Breton tells of the following exchange in a restaurant on April 10, 1934: a "poetic" waitress is beckoned by the bouncer: « Ici, l'Ondine! » [Here, Mermaid!]. She answers with an involuntary pun that delights the author: "Ah! oui, on le fait ici, l'on dine!" [Oh! yes, it's done here, one eats dinner!]. See also note 2 to "Zinnia-red eyes," above.

2. *Sagittaire en fer de lance:* word play on the sign of the zodiac, Sagittarius, and on the arrowhead, an aquatic plant (genus *Sagittaria)* with sagittal or lanceolate leaves.

"Your limbs go unfolding . . ."

1. In Roman times, copper mined in Cyprus was consecrated to Venus. Attracted to copper because of its resemblance to gold, the medieval alchemists associated the metal with the sign of Venus. Breton had an abiding fascination with alchemy.

"If I were you .."

1. One of the heroes of Ariosto's *Orlando furioso* (1516), Ruggiero rescues the maid Angelica from a sea monster.

2. In Greek legend, Danaë was imprisoned in a brass tower by her father Acrisius to forestall the realization of a prophecy that he would be killed by her son. Zeus appeared before her in a shower of gold, and she bore him a son, Perseus. Acrisius enclosed Danaë and Perseus in a chest which he threw into the sea, but it floated safely to land and the prophecy was eventually fulfilled.

3. *Survivre* harkens back to *vivre*, "living," line 18.

"Always for the first time"

1. Surrounded by fields of flowers and rose gardens, the town of Grasse in Provence is the capital of the French perfume industry.

2. *Miellée:* literally, "honeydew," the sticky sweet substance exuded by certain plants and flowers, here continuing the floral motif beginning in line 16 and extending through line 33.

3. A street in the ninth *arrondissement* of Paris which, at its northern end, crosses the rue Pigalle and becomes the rue Fontaine, where Breton resided (at no. 42) for many years.

4. *Hauts bas:* word play; literally, "high lows," as well as "tall stockings."

The Enchanted Well

1. *Boîte de nuit:* here rendered literally; possibly suggests a spittoon or chamber pot. The usual meaning is "night club."

2. *Fulgora:* a genus of homopterous insects, chiefly lantern flies.

3. Pteropus: a kind of fruit bat.

4. *Au fil de l'eau,* literally, "with the stream," and *Ophélie* are nearly homophonous.

5. Peter Ibbetson: a deranged murderer in the novel of the same name by George du Maurier (1891). The novel was translated into French by Raymond Queneau, a former surrealist.

Run-them-all

1. Feminized here in accordance with the feminine *acanthe.* Etymologically, the original Greek word means "spine" (cf. line 50). The acanthus motif used as an ornament of sculpted marble is suggested in line 54.

2. The personal and symbolic associations of the Tour Saint-Jacques—a medieval belfry in central Paris—are many (see note to "Vigilance," p. 291).

Fata Morgana

1. Fata Morgana: Italian for Morgan le Fay, of the Arthurian legend; a complex mirage occurring in the Strait of Messina on tranquil mornings when the rising sun strikes the smooth surface of the Mediterranean sea at a 45° angle. Objects on the Sicilian coast, such as ships, houses, men, and horses, are so magnified as to appear suspended in the air or on the water, often in mirror image.

2. A reference to the Camargue and its flocks of winged wildlife, most notably cranes and flamingoes. (Breton was staying in the vicinity of the Camargue during the time of the poem's composition.)

3. Gaspard de Coligny (1519–1572), whose statue looks down on passersby in the rue de Rivoli, led expeditions to Brazil and to Florida. He is chiefly known as a military leader, as adviser to Charles IX, and as a supporter of the Huguenot cause.

4. *Papier d'Arménie:* a thin, flameless, slow-burning aromatic paper used to rid the air of undesirable odors; unknown in the United States.

5. *Les chaussures les mieux accordées/Sur les paliers mordorés:* a multiple word play. *Accordées* is of course "matched" (as a pair of shoes) as well as "in tune" (suggested by *coup d'archet* [stroke of the bow] and the stringed instrument implied); the adjective *mordorés* [bronze] is here associated with *paliers* [landings] instead of with the normal *chaussures* [shoes].

6. Mount Knock-Farril (elevation 579 feet) in the southeast part of Ross and Cromarty County, Scotland, is crowned by a vitrified fort.

7. Viennese-born painter, instrumental in introducing surrealism to Mexico (1907-1959).

8. The *armoire à glace,* "mirror wardrobe" suggests a play on the word *glace* in its meaning of "ice," linked here to the skate alluded to in the preceding line.

9. The diamond set in a pane is similar to a watch indicating to the minute and in minute detail the temporal harmony of the spheres.

10. A notable example of broken syntax.

11. A reference to Horace Walpole's gothic novel *The Castle of Otranto* (1764), in which a massive plumed helmet symbolizes fate.

12. A deliberate substitution of kindred terms: *aiguillée,* "needleful" or "length of thread," for *aiguillage,* "rail switch" or "switching"; also a play on *aiguille folle,* "crazy compass needle."

13. *Taille:* a play on both meanings, the "cut" of a gemstone and the "size" of an object.

14. The verb *piper* means "to load" (dice) or "to lure" (birds by means of bird calls). Thus *pipé* refers back to the birds of the preceding line.

15. Lines 150–186 (in italics) are the transcription of a dream (Gérard Legrand, *André Breton en son temps,* pp. 106–107).

16. *All right is* in English in the original. It is thus rendered in French in the translation.

17. The *cigales* here are *cigales de mer,* "squillfishes" or "mantis shrimps."

18. A coinage, after the garden mignonette or *reseda odorata,* also known as *herbe d'amour.* The question was asked by Breton's daughter Aube just before or after the dream reported here (Legrand, *André Breton en son temps,* p. 107).

19. A reference to Nietzsche's last letter, dated January 6, 1889, addressed to Jakob Burckhardt from Turin. The letter documents the insanity that had just befallen its author. Nietzsche claims to have been born as King Victor Emmanuel II and identifies with two criminals, Prado and Chambige, whose separate trials in November 1888 attracted widespread

attention in the press. See F. Nietzsche, *Selected Letters*, trans. and ed. Christopher Middleton (Chicago, 1969), pp. 316, 347. *Astu* is a Greek word meaning "home town" or "city." The lines immediately following, 217–218, also have Nietzschean overtones.

20. Stones engraved to show a human body often capped by a rooster's head and inscribed with the magical word *Abraxas* in Greek letters, used as talismans in the Eastern Mediterranean beginning in the second century A.D. Their origin (whether Christian, pagan, or gnostic) is uncertain. The gnostic sect of Basilides is known to have worshipped the god Abraxas.

21. Queen of France (1371–1435), wife of Charles VI (1368–1422). This entire concluding section is a composite representation, in cinematic terms, of events that occurred during the reign of Charles VI, telescoping the years 1389–1408.

22. In italics, terminology of the cinema, as in a shooting script.

23. The heraldic emblem of Charles VI included a winged stag and a *rai de soleil* ("sun in his splendor").

24. Lines 266–272 allude to the documented circumstances surrounding Charles VI's first lapse into madness near Le Mans in August 1392.

25. *Le bal des ardents,* also known as the *bal des sauvages.* In 1393, on the occasion of a ball at the hôtel Saint-Paul in Paris, Charles VI, disguised as a wild man *(sauvage)* with five companions, narrowly escaped death after his highly flammable costume caught fire, accidentally ignited by a torch held by Louis, Duke of Orleans, his younger brother. The five other *sauvages* burned to death, hence the image of the burning bush *(buisson ardent)* in line 283.

26. In August 1389 a buffoon bearing a torch in each hand walked a tight-rope strung between one of the cathedral's towers and the roof of a house on the Saint-Michel bridge.

27. See note 25.

28. On November 23, 1407, Louis, Duke of Orleans, was assassinated by order of Jean sans Peur, Duke of Burgundy. Accounts of the event mention Louis' playing with a glove as he rode horseback.

29. The antipope Benedict XIII (1334–1424).

30. Valentine Visconti (1366–1408), wife of the Duke of Orleans. She adopted the motto cited in line 291 during her widowhood. Breton's designation of her as a queen rather than as a duchess is perhaps deliberate: the duchess' love for her husband stands in sharp contrast to Queen Isabel of Bavaria's reputed infidelity and scheming.

31. The marigold, emblem of Valentine Visconti. Clearly implied as well is *souci* in its Middle French meaning of "grief" or "sorrow."

Grade Crossing

1. Play on *pomme,* "apple," and on *pommes vapeur,* short for *pommes de terre à la vapeur,* "steamed potatoes."

The Dark Lantern

1. Also called a bull's-eye lantern, i.e., a lantern with a single opening, which may be closed to conceal the light. For Breton, the *lanterne sourde* symbolized the means of gaining access to the most private, innermost, nocturnal self.

2. *Piquer* here has the special meaning of "to cause spots" or "to eat away" as a result of rot or mildew. *Piquer la tente is* reminiscent of the idiomatic *piquer une tête,* "to pitch headlong," and *piquet de tente,* "tent peg."

3. A reference to *suichuka,* or flowers in water, i.e., especially prepared paper which blossoms into flowers when immersed in water. A celebrated instance of its metaphorical use appears in the opening section of Proust's *A la recherche du temps perdu (Remembrance of Things Past* or *In Search of Lost Time).*

4. *Souliers à la poulaine* are shoes with long pointed toes worn in the fourteenth and fifteenth centuries, following a fashion that originated in Poland.

5. *Pâmer* [to faint] is normally intransitive, as in English. A striking violation of usage and an example of post-rimbaldian poetic license.

"In Haiti at night . . ."

1. *Mornes,* "hills" or "bluffs," a creole term derived from the Spanish *morro* and used in the French Antilles.

2. Painter, born in Cuba in 1902. After living in Spain from 1923 to 1938, he moved to Paris and became a surrealist. In 1942 he returned to Cuba, then went to the United States.

3. *"Vèver"* or *vévé:* ritual diagram drawn on the ground with flour, coffee grounds, or ashes, in a voodoo ceremony, to summon the *loa* (spirit).

4. *Le loa Carrefour is* the deity or spirit particular to the town of Carrefour [Crossroads], which lies west of Port-au-Prince, Haiti. Elleguà (otherwise known as Elegbara or Alegua) is a Cuban deity.

Korwar

1. Korwars are sacred statues of Melanesia worshipped for the protective spirits that inhabit them. The poem clearly refers to a funerary statuette from Dutch New Guinea in Breton's collection of Oceanica, a photograph of which is reproduced in the catalog for an exhibition of Oceanic art *(Océanie,* Paris: Galerie Andrée Olive, June 7, 1948). In his foreword to the catalog, Breton writes about Oceanic art: "Les thèmes sont aériens, les plus chargés de spiritualité que je sache, les plus poignants aussi. . . . Océanie . . . de quel prestige ce mot n'aura-t-il pas joui dans le surréalisme. Il aura été un des grands éclusiers de notre cœur." [The themes are airy, the most spiritually charged that I know, the most poignant too . . . . Oceania . . . what prestige that word has enjoyed in surrealism! It is one of the great watersheds of the heart.] *(La Clé des champs, p.* 214)

2. *Ne pas être piqué des vers,* an idiomatic phrase meaning "to be first-rate" (literally, "not to be worm-eaten").

Uli

1. Ulis are statues representing ancient Oceanic chieftains. In Breton's possession was an Uli from New Ireland.

Dukduk

1. Name of a secret tribal society of New Britain, in Melanesia, whose ritual is founded on the cult of the sun; also an elongated mask used by its members in ceremonies.

2. In New Britain.

3. *Là-haut cône:* literally, "up there cone"; pun on Laocoön, priest of Apollo, who warned the Trojans not to touch the wooden horse fashioned by the Greeks during the Trojan War. While he was sacrificing to Poseidon at the seashore with his two sons, two serpents emerged from the water and crushed them.

4. *Gare:* another pun. The two meanings are "railway station" and "beware" or "look out!"

Tiki

1. Polynesian idol inhabited by protective spirits. Breton had in his possession two tikis, one in stone from the Marquesas Islands, the other in mother-of-pearl from New Zealand.

Rano Raraku

1. Volcano on Easter Island, site of numerous giant statues.

2. Allusion to the petroglyphs of Orongo, on Easter Island, which represent *hommes-oiseaux*, "bird-men."

3. *Volètent:* normal spelling would be *volettent.*

Seashell Sail

1. *Ecoute* is both the verb "listen," as in *écoute à la porte*, "listen at the door, eavesdrop," and a noun, the "sheet" of a sail.

2. A reference among many interspersed throughout this text to Rimbaud's prose poem from the *Illuminations*. Aube is the name of Breton's daughter, born in December 1935.

On the Road to San Romano

1. Title derived from Paolo Uccello's three panels depicting the rout of San Romano *(La rotta di San Romano,* ca. 1455), one of which hangs in the Louvre. Much admired by Breton, the painting portrays a battle that took place near Florence on June 1, 1432.

Persons in the Night Guided by Phosphorescent Snail Tracks

1. Titles of all twenty-two poems in *Constellations* are those of Joan Miró, for whose gouaches Breton composed the parallel texts.

2. Gérard de Nerval (1808–1855), author of *Aurélia;* Xavier Forneret (1809-1884), author of *Le Diamant de l'herbe,* known to his contemporaries as « l'homme noir »; Arthur Rimbaud (1854–1891), author of the *Illuminations* and *Une Saison en enfer.* All three are literary figures in the pantheon of surrealism's precursors.

3. A variety of feldspar, usually grey, noted for its iridescent qualities.

Women on the Beach

1. *Faire la roue* also designates the peacock spreading his tail.

2. *Abîme* and *sublime* are linked not only by rhyme but also by a common verticality.

Woman with Blond Underarm Combing Her Hair in the Starlight

1. Twelfth-century feudal château in eastern Brittany, noted for its thirteen towers.

2. *Que sous . . . clématite:* An extreme example of Breton's centrifugal or exploded syntax. Among the possible readings, the most "logical" that presents itself once the syntactical components are unscrambled is the following: "Le torrent qui bondit couleur de rouille à chaque détour du parc du château de Fougères aux treize tours par la grâce du geste qui découvre et recouvre le nid sournoisement tramé des vrilles de la clématite n'est pas plus confondant dans sa chute que sous le pouvoir du peigne cette masse fluide, mûrement brassée de sarrasin et d'avoine, tout au long épinglée de décharges électriques.» [The leaping rust-colored torrent at every turn of the grounds of the château of Fougères with its thirteen towers by the grace of the gesture that uncovers and covers over the slyly woven nest of the clematis tendrils is no more mingling in its fall than under the comb's sway this fluid mass, mellow-brewed with buckwheat and oats, pinned throughout with electrical discharges.]

Morning Star

1. *Frisante:* also "curling."

2. *Tes sillons grisollent:* suggests a spoonerism on *tes grillons s'isolent,* "your crickets isolate themselves." An example of the latent complicity of words, of pure verbal "love-making" (see Introduction, p. 24.

Injured Person

1. *Le fil des poignards:* the conventional phrase is *le fil de l'épée,* "the sword's edge."

2. Jan Potocki (1761–1815), Polish author of a fantastic tale written in French, *Manuscrit trouvé à Saragosse* [The Saragossa manuscript] (1804).

The Song of the Nightingale at Midnight and the Morning Rain

1. A genus of insects that includes the asparagus beetle.

The Awakening at Daybreak

1. *Cerfs-volants* can also be understood literally, as "flying stags."

2. In the late twelfth-century French chanson de geste *Huon de Bordeaux,* the hero, Huon, wins Esclarmonde, daughter of the emir of Babylon, thanks to the magical intervention of Oberon, the dwarf king.

3. That is, cries like a rutting stag. The term is rarer in English than the French *bramer,* but Breton is not averse to using arcane words, as is evident in many of his poems.

4. The visible tokens by which Huon proves that he has accomplished his deeds. They belong to Esclarmonde's father, the emir Gaudisse, whom Huon slays.

Women by the Shore of a Lake
Made Iridescent by a Passing Swan

1. *Elles s'y rendent* also suggests "there they yield" or "surrender."

2. *Fait ruche* has the ring of an idiomatic expression (such as *fait rage,* "rages," or *fait mouche,* "strikes home," "scores a bull's eye") but is a coinage.

3. *Luxe and volupté* in association are inevitably reminiscent of Baudelaire's famous line "Luxe, calme, et volupté » (from « L'Invitation au voyage").

"The experience (active-passive) of listening . . ."

1. First published in *Minotaure* in December 1933, later included in *Point du jour* (1934).

2. A reference to the poem « Ce que dit la Bouche d'ombre » [What the mouth of shadows says] in Victor Hugo's *Les Contemplations*. From the "mouth of shadows" (equated by Breton with the unconscious) emanate cosmic utterances.

The Life and Works
of André Breton

A CHRONOLOGY

(Asterisks mark dates of publication of Breton's works.)

1896–1906. André Breton born in Tinchebray (Normandy) on February 19, 1896. Early childhood spent with maternal grandfather in Saint-Brieuc (Brittany). Settles in Pantin, near Paris, with family (1906).

1906–1913. Secondary studies in private school, the Collège Chaptal. Introduced to works of Baudelaire, Mallarmé, and Huysmans by one of his teachers. Discovers the paintings of Gustave Moreau. Begins premedical studies.

1914. First visit to Paul Valéry. Their friendship continues through 1922. Publishes three poems in *La Phalange*. Reads Rimbaud during summer.

1915. Drafted; after military training at Pontivy, assigned to duty in Nantes as nurse. Writes first letter to Apollinaire.

1916. Meets Jacques Vaché. While on leave, visits Apollinaire at hospital in Paris. Late July: reassigned to psychiatric center in Saint-Dizier; studies psychoanalysis, especially the theories of Freud; takes great interest in mental patients, applies free-association methods to them.

1917. Nonresident assistant at neurological center in Paris. Sees Apollinaire often; meets Philippe Soupault, Louis Aragon, Pierre Reverdy; publishes in *Nord-Sud*.

1918. Corresponds with, then meets, Paul Eluard. Reads *Les Chants de Maldoror* of Lautréamont (Isidore Ducasse).

1919. Jacques Vaché commits suicide. B. Starts review *Littérature* with Aragon and Soupault, publishes Lautréamont's *Poésies*. Discovers automatic writing. Its practice leads to *Les Champs magnétiques*, written with Soupault in this year.
* *Mont de piété.*

1920.	B. and editors of *Littérature* rally to cause of Dada. B. befriends Tristan Tzara and Benjamin Péret, participates in Dada happenings.
	* Les Champs magnétiques (with Soupault).
1921.	B. and his friends become disillusioned with Dada. B. marries Simone Kahn. Visits Freud in Vienna.
1922.	After an unsuccessful attempt at reforming Dada, B. breaks with it. With friends, engages in activities designed to tap resources of the unconscious: dream narration, hypnotic sleep, hallucinatory trances, automatic writing. Because these take an alarming turn, they are terminated after a few months. In Barcelona for a Francis Picabia exhibition, B. becomes acquainted with work of Joan Miró, gives lecture on modernism laying groundwork for surrealism. Champions work of Giorgio de Chirico, Marcel Duchamp, Man Ray, Max Ernst.
1923.	B. and his friends experiment with games of chance. A Dadaist spectacle leads to violent confrontation between emerging surrealist group and Dadaists, resulting in Dada's demise. Impressed by poetry of Saint-Pol Roux, B. dedicates *Clair de terre* to him.
	* Clair de terre.
1924.	As a result of violent attack against Anatole France published under title *Un Cadavre*, B. loses position as librarian and advisor to book collector and fashion designer Jacques Doucet. The first issue of *La Révolution surréaliste*, edited by Pierre Naville and Péret, appears in December. A Surrealist Research Bureau opens in Paris.
	* Les Pas perdus.
	* Manifeste du surréalisme. Poisson soluble.
1925.	B. assumes editorship of *La Révolution surréaliste*. Impressed by Leon Trotsky's book on Lenin. Participates in several surrealist scandals.
	* Introduction au Discours sur le peu de réalité.
1926.	Opening of Galerie Surréaliste. B. encounters Nadja, embodiment of an innately surrealistic *âme errante* [errant soul].
1927.	B. joins Communist Party out of revolutionary idealism, a phase in his lifelong belief in libertarian principles and social emancipation. Has no illusions about petty inadequacies of party, which he soon leaves. Engages in ideological debates with Soupault, Antonin Artaud, André Masson. Writes *Nadja*. His former mentor Valéry enters Académie Française, to B.'s intense disgust.
1928.	** Nadja.*
	* Le Surréalisme et la peinture.
1929.	A difficult year for B. owing to unrequited romantic attachment to "X" (Suzanne Musard), and to conflicts resulting from his ideological position. The fiercely contentious *Second Manifeste* appears in *La Révolution surréaliste*, with many references to occult sciences, judged by B. to be compatible with Hegelian dialectics. B. and his wife separate.

1930.   B. attacked by ex-surrealists in libelous pamphlet, *Un Cadavre.* With Aragon, starts new review, *Le Surréalisme A.S.D.L.R.* [= *au service de la révolution*]. First showing of film *L'Age d'or* by Luis Buñuel and Salvador Dalí causes scandal.
* *Second Manifeste du surréalisme.*
* *L'Immaculée Conception* (with Eluard).

1931.   Still despondent from unhappy love affair with Suzanne Musard, B. continues some political activity, albeit against increasing opposition of Communist Party.
* *L'Union libre.*

1932.   B. breaks with Aragon, whose primary allegiance lies with Communist Party rather than surrealist principles.
* *Le Revolver à cheveux blancs.* [Includes a significant foreword, "Il y aura une fois. »]
* *Les Vases communicants.*

1933.   B.'s increasingly independent stance and Trotskyite views cause his expulsion from Association of Revolutionary Writers and Artists. Collaborates in creation of new review, *Minotaure;* soon becomes its guiding light. In essay "Le Message automatique, » B. concedes failings of automatic writing.

1934·   On February 6, date of attempted coup by French royalist, fascist, and communist groups, B. takes steps to rally as many intellectuals as possible to defense of republican freedoms. Publishes important essay "La Beauté sera convulsive." On May 29, encounters the "scandalously beautiful" Jacqueline Lamba, who becomes his second wife on August 14.
* *Qu'est-ce que le surréalisme?*
* *Point du jour.*
* *L'Air de l'eau.*

1935.   B. lectures in Prague, Brussels, and Canary Islands on occasion of surrealist exhibitions. Having slapped Soviet writer Ilya Ehrenburg in the face for his attacks on surrealism, B. is refused participation in International Congress for Defense of Culture. His friend René Crevel attempts to reverse decision, fails, and commits suicide. B. completes surrealism's break with Communist Party, condemns Stalinism. In December, birth of B.'s daughter Aube, delivered by Dr. Pierre Mabille, a friend versed in the occult.
* *Position politique du surréalisme.*

1936.   B. lectures at surrealist exhibition in London; reacts strongly against Moscow Trials and Spanish Civil War.

1937.   B. manages Gradiva, a surrealist gallery; joins new editorial board of *Minotaure.*
* *L'Amour fou.*

1938.   International surrealist exhibition opens in Paris. B. publishes admiring essay on Freud, then threatened by Nazi invasion of Austria. On visit to Mexico, B. lectures on art, has frequent conversations with Trotsky, with whom he drafts manifesto promoting total artistic freedom, "For an Independent Revolutionary Art" (text bears signatures of B. and Diego Rivera). B. breaks with Eluard.
* *Dictionnaire abrégé du surréalisme.*

1939–1940. Mobilized as medical aide, B. is assigned to aviation school in Poitiers; demobilized in 1940; stays with P. Mabille in Salon-de-Provence, then in Marseilles at "Air-Bel" villa placed at disposal of artists and writers by American Committee for Aid to Intellectuals. With several friends, B. resumes surrealist activities; writes *Fata Morgana,* his longest poem.

1940. ** Anthologie de l'humour noir.* [Publication suspended by Vichy authorities.]
* Pleine marge.

1941. Sails for Martinique with Jacqueline and Aube. Discovers poetry of Aimé Césaire, whom he meets. In August, arrives in New York.
* Fata Morgana. [Publication denied by Vichy.]

1942–1944. While earning his living as announcer for Voice of America, B. collaborates with old and new friends (Duchamp, Ernst, Masson, Matta, Tanguy) in surrealist publications (the review *VVV*) and exhibitions. Lectures to students at Yale on status of surrealism between two world wars (December 1942). Meets Elisa Bindhoff (1943); they spend summer and fall of 1944 on Gaspé peninsula, Canada, where he writes *Arcane 17.*

1945. B. visits several Indian reservations in Arizona and New Mexico. Divorces Jacqueline in Reno, marries Elisa. Writes bulk of *Ode à Charles Fourier.* Visits Haiti, is welcomed by P. Mabille, now cultural attaché there. B.'s lectures on freedom and arts contribute to student disorders, political turmoil.
* Arcane 17.
* Le Surréalisme et la peinture [new enlarged ed.].

1946. B. returns to France. At meeting in honor of Artaud (June 7), states opposition to then fashionable notion of *engagement,* re-affirms utopian goal of transforming life by unlocking potential of human psyche. During postwar period, B. maintains uncompromising stance of nonpartisan independence, keeping his distance from Sartrean existentialism, Communist ideology, and spiritualist doctrines.
* Yves Tanguy.

1947. In guest lecture at Sorbonne, Tzara declares that surrealism has run its course and that its goals have been preempted by Communism. B. intervenes, blows are exchanged. International surrealist exhibition at Galerie Maeght, Paris.
* Ode à Charles Fourier.
* Martinique charmeuse de serpents.

1948–1949. B. pursues activities on many fronts; contributes with others to the review *Néon*; draws attention to Malcolm de Chazal's *Sens plastique*; exposes literary forgery of *La Chasse spirituelle,* falsely attributed to Rimbaud.
* La Lampe dans l'horloge (1948).
* Poèmes (1948).
* Flagrant Délit (1949)

1950. With Péret, edits *Almanach surréaliste du demi-siècle.* On visit to Quercy, is charmed by village of Saint-Cirq-Lapopie near Cahors; soon thereafter purchases old house, to become his summer retreat.
* Anthologie de l'humour noir [new expanded ed.].

1951–1952. Dissension in surrealist ranks owing to Michel Carrouges' avowal of his Catholic faith after publication (1950) of his book *André Breton et les données fondamentales du surréalisme*. B. publishes articles in *Arts* (attacking Camus for ideas presented in *L'Homme révolté* and condemning Stalinist principles of socialist realism), also in *Le Libertaire* and *Médium*. Attends lectures by René Alleau on alchemy which strengthen his long-held belief that surrealist processing of language is akin to alchemical transmutation of matter. In series of radio interviews (February–June 1952), B. casts long retrospective look at his life and work.

    * *Entretiens* (1952).

1953–1958. B. champions new artists, writers, and art forms, shows ever increasing interest in primitive art; protests against Soviet invasion of Hungary; directs new review, *Le Surréalisme, même*; opposes advent of Gaullist regime and Algerian war; defends conscientious objectors.

    * *La Clé des champs* (1953)

1959–1961. International surrealist exhibition on theme of eroticism held in Paris. B. active in organizing exhibitions in New York and Milan.

    * *Constellations* (1959).

    * *Le La* (1961).

1962–1965. B. contributes to new review, *La Brèche*. Promotes primitive art in its many forms. Prepares eleventh international surrealist exhibition, directed against consumer society.

    * *Le Surréalisme et la peinture* [new expanded ed.].

1966. Declining health. After brief visit to Brittany, B. goes to Saint-Cirq-Lapopie; brought back to Paris gravely ill on September 27 for hospitalization; dies the next day. On October 1, B. is buried in Batignolles cemetery. His obituary notice is worded:

André Breton
1896–1966
Je cherche l'or du temps

("I seek the gold of time," a phrase from his *Introduction au Discours sur le peu de réalité*.)

Selected Bibliography

Works by André Breton
Critical Editions in French

L'Amour fou. Paris: Gallimard, Collection "Folio," 1976.
Anthologie de l'humour noir. Paris: Pauvert, 1966.
Arcane 17, enté d'Ajours. Paris: Union Générale d'Editions, 1965.
Clair de terre. Paris: Gallimard, Collection « Poésie, » 1966.
La Clé des champs. Paris: Pauvert, 1967.
Entretiens. Paris: Gallimard, Collection « Idées, » 1969.
Manifestes du surréalisme. Paris: Pauvert, 1962.
Nadja. Paris: Gallimard, Collection "Folio," 1972.
Oeuvres Complètes. Paris: Gallimard (Pléiade), ed. Marguerite Bonnet, Etienne-Alain Hubert, with Philippe Bernier, Marie-Claire Dumas, and José Pierre. Three of the projected four volumes have appeared, 1988–2006.
Les Pas perdus. Paris: Gallimard, Collection « Idées, » 1969.
Perspective cavalière. Paris: Gallimard, 1970.
Poèmes. Paris: Gallimard, 1948.
Point du jour. Paris: Gallimard, Collection « Idées, 1970.
Signe ascendant. Paris: Gallimard, Collection « Poésie, » 1968.
Le Surréalisme et la peinture. Paris: Gallimard, 1965.
Les Vases communicants. Paris: Gallimard, Collection « Idées, » 1970.
Manifestes du surrealisme d'André Breton. Paris: Gallimard, 2002.

Works by André Breton
in English Translation

Andre Breton: Selection (Poets for the Millennium.) Edited by Mark Polizzotti. Berkeley: University of California Press, 2004.
Break of Day. Translated by Mark Polizzotti and Mary Ann Caws. Lincoln: University of Nebraska Press, 1999.
Communicating Vessels. Translated by Mary Ann Caws and Geoffrey Harris. Lincoln: University of Nebraska Press, 1991.
Conversations: The Autobiography of Surrealism. (Conversations with Andre Parinaud and others.) Translated by Mark Polizzotti. New York: Paragon House, 1993.
Earthlight. Translated by Bill Zavatsky and Zack Rogow. Los Angeles: Sun & Moon Press, 1993. Revised edition, Boston: Black Widow Press, 2014.

The Lost Steps: Les Pas Perdus (French Modernist Library) Translated by Mark Polizzotti. Lincoln: University of Nebraska Press, 1997.

Mad Love. Translated by Mary Ann Caws. Lincoln: University of Nebraska Press, 1987.

Manifestos of Surrealism. Translated by Richard Seaver and Helen Lane. Ann Arbor: University of Michigan Press, 1969.

My Heart through which Her Heart has Passed: Poems of Love and Desperation. Translated by Mark Polizzotti. Paris: Alyscamps Press; 2nd edition (2001).

Nadja. Translated by Richard Howard. New York: Grove, 1960.

Poems of André Breton: A Bilingual Anthology. Edited and Translated by Jean-Pierre Cauvin and Mary Ann Caws. Austin: University of Texas Press, 1982. Revised edition; Boston: Black Widow Press, 2006.

Selected Poems. Translated by Kenneth White. London: Jonathan Cape, 1969.

Surrealism and Painting. Translated by Simon Watson Taylor. New York: Harper and Row, 1972. repr. Boston: Museum of Fine Arts, 2002 (introduction, Mark Polizzotti).

What is Surrealism? Selected Writings. Edited and translated by Franklin Rosemont. New York: Monad Press, 1978.

Selected Critical Works on André Breton in English

Alquié, Ferdinand. *The Philosophy of Surrealism*. Translated by Bernard Waldrop. Ann Arbor: University of Michigan Press, 1965.

Aspley, Keith. *André Breton the Poet*. Glasgow, University of Glasgow Press, 1989.

Balakian, Anna. *André Breton: Magus of Surrealism*. New York: Oxford University Press, 1971.

Browder, Clifford. *André Breton: Arbiter of Surrealism*. Geneva: Droz, 1967.

Carrouges, Michel. *André Breton and the Basic Concepts of Surrealism*. Translated by Maura Prendergast. University, Ala.: University of Alabama Press, 1974.

Caws, Mary Ann. *André Breton*. New York: Twayne, 1973; revised ed., *André Breton Revisited*, 1996.

———— *The Poetry of Dada and Surrealism: Aragon, Breton, Tzara, Eluard, and Desnos*. Princeton: Princeton University Press, 1971.

———— *Surrealism and the Literary Imagination: A Study of Gaston Bachelard and André Breton*. The Hague: Mouton, 1966.

Ellenwood, William Ray. *André Breton and Freud*. Ann Arbor: University Microfilms, 1972.

Matthews, J. H. *André Breton*. New York: Columbia University Press, 1967.

Polizzotti, Mark. *Revolution of the Mind: The Life of André Breton*. New York: Farrar, Straus and Giroux, 1995. Updated and augmented edition, Boston: Black Widow Press, 2009.

Thirion, André. *Revolutionaries Without a Revolution*, translated by Joachim Neugroschel. New York: Macmillan, 1975.

Selected Critical Works on André Breton in French

Alexandrian, Sarane. *André Breton par lui-même.* Paris: Seuil, 1971.

—— *Le Surréalisme et le rêve.* Paris: Gallimard, 1974.

Audoin, Philippe. *Breton.* Paris: Gallimard, 1970.

Benezet Mathieu. *André Breton: Rêveur définitif—essai de lire.* Paris: Editions du Rocher, 1996.

Blachère, Jean-Claude. *Les totems d'André Breton: Surréalisme et primitivisme litteraire.* Paris: L'Harmattan, 1996.

Bonnet, Marguerite. *André Breton: Naissance de l'aventure surréaliste.* Paris: Corti, 1975.

—— *Les Critiques de notre temps et Breton.* Paris: Garnier, 1974.

Duits, Charles. *André Breton: a-t-il dit passe.* Paris: Maurice Nadeau, 1998.

Durozoi, Gérard, and Bernard Lecherbonnier. *André Breton: L'Ecriture surréaliste.* Paris: Larousse, Collection « Thèmes et Textes, » 1974.

Gracq, Julien. *André Breton: Quelques aspects de l'écrivain.* Paris: Jose Corti, 1989.

Graulle, Cristophe. *André Breton et l'humour noir: une révolte supérieure de l'esprit.* Paris: L'Harmattan, 2001.

Legrand, Gérard. *André Breton en son temps.* Paris: Soleil, 1976.

—— *Breton.* Paris: Belfond, 1977.

Polizzotti, Mark. *André Breton.* Paris: Gallimard, 1999.

Vielwahr, André. *Sous le signe des contradictions: André Breton de 1913 à 1924.* Paris: Nizet, 1980.

Selected General Works Concerning Surrealism in English

Brandon, Ruth. *Surreal Lives: The Surrealists, 1917-1945.* New York: Macmillan, 1999

Caws, Mary Ann. *The Surrealist Look: An Erotics of Encounter.* Cambridge and London: M.I.T. Press, 1997.

—— *Surrealism and the Art of Display.* Wexner Center, Surrealism exhibition, Fall, 1997.

—— *Surrealism.* London and New York: Phaidon (Themes and Movements Series), 2004.

—— *The Surrealist Painters and Poets.* Editor and co-translator. Cambridge and London: M.I.T. Press, 2001.

—— *Surrealist Love Poems.* Editor and co-translator. London: Tate Publishing and the University of Chicago Press, 2002; 2005.

Durozoi, Gerard. *History of the Surrealist Movement.* Translated by Alison Anderson. Chicago: University of Chicago Press, 2003.

Gershman, Herbert. *The Surrealist Revolution in France.* Ann Arbor: University of Michigan Press, 1968.

Gale, Matthew. *Dada and Surrealism*. London: Phaidon, 1997
Levy, Julien, ed., *Surrealism*. New York: Da Capo Press, 1995. Reprint of 1936 limited edition.
Nadeau, Maurice. *The History of Surrealism*. Translated by Richard Howard. 1967; Cambridge: Bellknap, 1989.
Sawin, Martica. *Surrealism in Exile and the Beginning of the New York School*. Cambridge and London; M.I.T. Press, 2001
Surrealism: Desire Unbound. Edited by Vince Gille, Jennifer Mundy. London: Tate, 2001

Bibliographic Work

Sheringham, Michael. *André Breton: A Bibliography*. London: Grant and Cutler, Research Bibliographies and Checklists, 2, 1972. (A complete bibliography of works by and about Breton through 1971.)
———. *André Breton: A Bibliography Supplement*. No. 1. 1972–1989. NY: D.S. Brewer, 1992.

TITLES FROM BLACK WIDOW PRESS

TRANSLATION SERIES

A Life of Poems, Poems of a Life
by Anna de Noailles. Translator: Norman
R. Shapiro. Introduction: Catherine Perry.

Approximate Man and Other Writings by
Tristan Tzara. Translator: Mary Ann Caws.

Art Poétique by Guillevic.
Translator: Maureen Smith.

The Big Game by Benjamin Péret.
Translator: Marilyn Kallet.

Capital of Pain by Paul Eluard.
Translators: Mary Ann Caws, Patricia Terry,
and Nancy Kline.

Chanson Dada: Selected Poems by
Tristan Tzara. Translator: Lee Harwood.

*Essential Poems and Writings of
Joyce Mansour: A Bilingual Anthology*
Translator: Serge Gavronsky.

Essential Poems and Prose of Jules Laforgue
Translator: Patricia Terry

*Essential Poems and Writings of Robert Desnos:
A Bilingual Anthology*
Translator: Mary Ann Caws

EyeSeas (Les Ziaux)
by Raymond Queneau. Translators:
Daniela Hurezanu and Stephen Kessler.

Furor and Mystery & Other Writings
by René Char. Translators: Mary Ann Caws
and Nancy Kline.

*Guarding the Air:
Selected Poems of Gunnar Harding*
Translator: Roger Greenwald.

The Inventor of Love & Other Writings
by Gherasim Luca. Translators: Julian
& Laura Semilian. Introduction: Andrei
Codrescu. Essay: Petre Răileanu.

La Fontaine's Bawdy by Jean de La Fontaine.
Translator: Norman R. Shapiro.

Last Love Poems of Paul Eluard
Translator: Marilyn Kallet.

Love, Poetry (L'amour la poésie)
by Paul Eluard. Translator: Stuart Kendall.

Poems of André Breton: A Bilingual Anthology
Translators: Jean-Pierre Cauvin and
Mary Ann Caws.

Poems of A.O. Barnabooth by Valéry Larbaud.
Translators: Ron Padgett and Bill Zavatsky.

Poems of Consummation by Vicente
Aleixandre. Translator: Stephen Kessler

Préversities: A Jacques Prévert Sampler
Translator: Norman R. Shapiro.

The Sea and Other Poems by Guillevic.
Translator: Patricia Terry. Introduction:
Monique Chefdor.

Selected Prose and Poetry of Jules Supervielle
Translators: Nancy Kline, Patricia Terry, and
Kathleen Micklow.

To Speak, to Tell You? Poems by Sabine
Sicaud. Translator: Norman R. Shapiro.
Introduction: Odile Ayral-Clause.

forthcoming translations

Earthlight (Claire de Terre) by André Breton.
Translators: Bill Zavatsky and Zack Rogrow
(new and revised edition)

Fables for the Modern Age by Pierre Coran.
Editor/translator: Norman R. Shapiro.
Illustrator: Olga Pastuchiv.

Pierre Reverdy: Poems Early to Late
Translators: Mary Ann Caws and
Patricia Terry.

*Boris Vian Invents Boris Vian:
A Boris Vian Reader*
Translator: Julia Older.

MODERN POETRY SERIES

ABC of Translation by Willis Barnstone

An Alchemist with One Eye on Fire
by Clayton Eshleman

Anticline by Clayton Eshleman

Archaic Design by Clayton Eshleman

Backscatter: New and Selected Poems
by John Olson

The Caveat Onus by Dave Brinks

City Without People: The Katrina Poems
by Niyi Osundare

Concealments and Caprichos
by Jerome Rothenberg

Crusader-Woman by Ruxandra Cesereanu.
Translator: Adam J. Sorkin. Introduction:
Andrei Codrescu.

Curdled Skulls: Poems of Bernard Bador
Translators: Bernard Bador and
Clayton Eshleman.

Endure: Poems by Bei Dao. Translators:
Clayton Eshleman and Lucas Klein.

Exile is My Trade: A Habib Tengour Reader
Translator: Pierre Joris.

Eye of Witness: A Jerome Rothenberg Reader
Heriberto Yepez & Jerome Rothenberg

Fire Exit by Robert Kelly

Forgiven Submarine by Ruxandra Cesereanu
and Andrei Codrescu

from stone this running by Heller Levinson

The Grindstone of Rapport:
A Clayton Eshleman Reader

Larynx Galaxy by John Olson

The Love That Moves Me by Marilyn Kallet

Memory Wing by Bill Lavender

Packing Light: New and Selected Poems
by Marilyn Kallet

The Present Tense of the World:
Poems 2000–2009 by Amina Saïd.
Translator: Marilyn Hacker.

The Price of Experience by Clayton Eshleman

The Secret Brain: Selected Poems 1995–2012
by Dave Brinks

Signal from Draco: New and Selected Poems
by Mebane Robertson

forthcoming modern poetry

An American Unconscious
by Mebane Robertson

Barzakh (Poems 2000–2012) by Pierre Joris

Funny Way of Staying Alive
by Willis Barnstone

The Hexagon by Robert Kelly

Memory by Bernadette Mayer

Penetralia by Clayton Eshleman

Soraya (Sonnets) by Anis Shivani

LITERARY THEORY / BIOGRAPHY SERIES

Revolution of the Mind:
The Life of André Breton
by Mark Polizzotti

Clayton Eshleman: The Whole Art
Edited by Stuart Kendall. *(forthcoming)*

Barbaric Vast & Wild: A Gathering of Outside
and Subterranean Poetry (Poems/Millennium,
vol 5) Edited by Jerome Rothenberg and John
Bloomberg. *(forthcoming)*

WWW.BLACKWIDOWPRESS.COM

Jean-Pierre Cauvin, Ph.D. is Professor of French at the University of Texas at Austin. He has written several books and numerous articles on topics including French poetry and Surrealism.

Mary Ann Caws, Ph.D., is Distinguished Professor of English, French, and Comparative Literature at the Graduate School of The City University of New York. She is the author, translator, and editor of numerous books and publications on the major figures of both Dada and Surrealism.

All Black Widow Press titles are printed on acid-free paper. Manufactured in the United States of America.

www.blackwidowpress.com

This book was set in Adobe Caslon Pro. The titling font is Aculida, a modernistic typeface used by many of the Dadaists in their typographic artworks.